Are You Adding Or Multiplying at Christmas?

Your Church Can Change Your Community in 25 Days

PASTOR GUY MELTON

ISBN 978-0-9883311-3-6 *paperback*

Editing and formatting by ChristianEditingandDesign.com

Contents

Dedication

It is only appropriate that I dedicate this book to the hundreds of staff and volunteers who have made Christmas at the Oasis such an incredible tradition in South Florida. It is truly a team effort. It outgrew me twenty years ago, but my fellow church members have taken it to a new level of reaching our community.

Thank you, Oasis staff, for putting up with endless meetings, vision lists (that are ten times what we can accomplish), and July workdays in ninety-degree weather while playing Christmas music.

Thanks to all our Oasis volunteers who put in hundreds (or even thousands) of hours. To you who climb trees, string lights, fix displays, greet, and even work from February through December on this passion that began with a little kid in Tampa, Florida.

Thank you for making it possible.

I love you, Oasis.

For we are God's handiwork, created in
Christ Jesus to do good works, which God
prepared in advance for us to do.

— Ephesians 2:10

Preface

This is the third book I said I would never write. After all, I am a pastor, not a writer. My heart is to pastor people, not to sit at a computer alone for days, writing to people I may never meet. Some people won't want to read it. Some may read it but not grasp the essence.

It was after years of ministry—almost forty at the time—that God first told me He wanted me to write a book about my Miami-to-New York City bike ride to raise funds for the people of Haiti. He had long before placed on my heart the vision and burden to come alongside the children, families, and pastors of Haiti. But now, amid a recession in the late 2000s, doing that seemed impossible.

Through a very clear word from God, I was compelled to ride a bicycle from Miami to New York City and ask people to pledge. That resulted in $750,000 invested in thousands of lives in Haiti ten years later. God's call came during the ride: "Write a book." I argued, complained, and finally said, "Okay. Only if I can raise another $100,000 for Haiti." That is how the book *Lessons FROM THE Road: Moving From The Mundane To The Miraculous* came about.

We never sold a book, but we were able to raise almost $150,000 from it. (Oasis church members sponsored books that were later given away.)

He had kept His word, and I had kept mine.

Years later, God impressed on my heart the need to lead our church into a deeper life of prayer. Prayer has always been a weak spot in my spiritual life, and I have found this to be true for most believers. For over thirteen years, I have been writing a weekly devotional for our Pastor's Prayer Partners, a group of members who pray for the church and its needs. Each devotional led me to read, study, and wrestle with prayer issues in my own life. The short end of the story is that the church council has graciously and generously given me a month each summer to write and study for future sermons and other projects. This set-apart time allowed me to write the second book I said I would never write. That book came out of years of devotionals on prayer and turned into a 365-day devotional. And so, the book *Brown Bag Prayers* became a reality. People reach out to me almost daily and tell me how much it has meant to them. Their texts, messages, and sometimes in-person conversations have been a source of real encouragement, making the pain of writing and doing what is so far out of my comfort zone worthwhile.

This book, the third, is another labor of love, pain, and great passion about something else God has called me to do, one of the highlights in my over forty years of full-time pastoral ministry.

I invite you along on a journey that began long before I became a pastor. In fact, it began when I was only five years old. I hope it may nudge you and your church in a positive way. It is my story seen from the perspective of Christmas. But it is not just my story. It also belongs to thousands of others who have called Oasis Church their home and the many thousands who have experienced Christmas at the Oasis (CATO) over the last twenty-five years.

CHAPTER 1

My Love Story with Christmas

"You are the light of the world. A town
built on a hill cannot be hidden."

— Matthew 5:14

My primary goal in writing this book is to paint a picture of one of the greatest opportunities for outreach during twenty-five days in December, something *any* church can accomplish. The gospel can be shared during Christmas with more people than at any other time of the year, even more than at Easter.

Many of us love Christmas. Without a doubt, it is the most beloved of all holidays in America. It's the holiday when people spend money more freely than at any other time. Hands down, more people participate in it than in any other celebration during the year. People do not have to be religious to love Christmas. So, it is a great opportunity for churches that want to share the good news with those in their community who will not attend church. Their love for Christmas gives churches a ripe opportunity to connect with them.

But first, let me take you back to the beginning.

My love for Christmas started when I was a small child. I was born 250 miles north of where I have spent my entire life since my family moved from Tampa to South Florida. I can remember as a small boy loving to go with our family to see Christmas lights. But the one picture in my mind that has impacted me until this day was a lake in an affluent neighborhood in Tampa called something like Christmas Card Lane. (Of course, to a poor kid, any neighborhood could have seemed affluent, but years later, I went back to confirm it.)

Beautifully lit houses surrounded the lake. The lakefront homes had large Christmas cards on them. They used something that looked like four-by-eight-foot pieces of plywood that contained messages of hope and love—and the story of Christmas. They were in every shape, size, and color. To small children, they seemed to have every conceivable light on them. In the middle of the lake, more lit-up cards floated on a barge. That's how my love of Christmas began. That scene remains indelibly etched in my mind's eye. And for several years at our Oasis Christmas display, our Bible-study groups and ministries re-created that scene (without the lake and fancy homes, of course).

I also remember how little we had at Christmas. Let us move from the affluent neighborhood that displayed these ornate life-size Christmas cards to my community, a sleepy suburb of Tampa called Temple Heights, across from what at the time was a Budweiser brewery (now a theme park called Busch Gardens). We lived in a small house. Actually, we made our home in at least three small houses during different times, all in the same neighborhood surrounding the brewery. I guess we moved often because my dad, who drank a lot, probably drank up the rent. I recall we even raised pigs in one of those little wooden houses down a dirt road and within eyesight of the brewery.

It was that backdrop that began to mold my love for Christmas.

With little money, our family didn't buy a live Christmas tree until Christmas Eve. By then, there were no live trees worth having, and if they were still on the lot, well, they were greatly discounted "Charlie Brown" trees. But that was what we got, and I loved it, not realizing we simply did not have the money to buy a tree early. That experience set the stage for our greatest outreach and mission project ever during Christmas at the Oasis, a project that is now associated with an Oasis Church Guinness World Record—one of two records our church holds for Christmas. (More about the world records in a later chapter.)

My love for Christmas had been born and flourished without any outside influences. That is, until my grandmother sent us a lot of outdoor lights from her old house when she and my grandfather moved into a retirement home. Ah, the kid with no money but now lots of lights.

I began to light our little house, and from there, after moving to South Florida, I can even remember buying a little nativity set for one dollar from the neighborhood Kmart. It would cost about ten dollars in today's money. That little nativity—minus a sheep and a donkey—can still be seen each year at our Guinness World Record nativity display. Thanks to my mom, who never threw anything away, my first nativity is still around to remind me where my love for Christmas began.

This love continued to grow. I added things to our little house in every community we lived in. We may have had the smallest and simplest house in the neighborhood, but it always had more lights than any other.

My dad eventually left, and as a single mom, my mother could not afford lights, so I would save up and buy them myself. Until 2020 when we moved, I still had some of the C-9 lights my grandmother had given me in the early 1960s, and they still worked, even though I had retired them many years before for fear they might burn down our house.

Even after I left home and married, my love for Christmas led to many annual family traditions. The joy of finding the best-decorated homes in our community and visiting them had become implanted when I was still in my mom's home and continued to be so important to me and my family after I married. In November, as soon as the newspaper or TV stations would list the best displays in South Florida, we would start to map our plans. These adventures started in our neighborhood, but over the years, they spread out from South Miami, all the way north to West Palm Beach. I could list so many of my favorite displays! I can still see them as if it were yesterday.

The one that influenced Oasis Church the most was the old *National Inquirer* tree in Lantana in Palm Beach County. Our family Christmas treks have expanded in the last twenty-five years since beginning Christmas at the Oasis. I have gone all over the United States, from California to New York and everywhere in between. The latest jaunt was to Canada for one of the great light displays of our northern friends. Each trip renews my love for Christmas and gives me at least one new idea for next year (although sometimes I come back with twenty-five). My poor sons. I cannot imagine what they thought as I dragged them all over South Florida looking at *one more* house. They love Christmas in their own ways, and that makes it all worthwhile, at least for me.

Up to the beginning of CATO, my love for Christmas had been a family and personal experience. But a cataclysmic event opened the door for our church's outreach, which has continued for almost thirty years.

The Mall Bans Jesus

*A person's heart plans his way, but
the Lord determines his steps.*

—Proverbs 16:9 CSB

Christmas at the Oasis began in a small and unusual way during our second year as a church. I wish I could say I had planned this incredible outreach and launched it, but I cannot. It has been a God thing all along.

The truth is, we had all kinds of plans when we launched Oasis Church, which was then called First Baptist Church of Pembroke Pines.

It was a small church of just over a hundred people when God did something no one saw coming, and yet He had prepared me for it decades before as a little kid. Only two years old and growing in a young blooming city, the church ended up in the middle of a firestorm.

Oasis Church began in the fall of 1991 in a little trailer with eleven members. We called it our core group, assembled from two area churches—the First Baptist Church of West Hollywood and the First Baptist Church of Ojus. The West Hollywood church was my home church; I grew up there and served on the staff for thirteen years.

It grew me, nurtured me, loved me through our family's tumultuous times with my alcoholic father, and it eventually sent me out to plant a new church in a new community. First Baptist Church of Ojus was a tiny declining church long past its heyday in a neighborhood that looked nothing like it once had when the church had thrived. But it had a pastor, Jim Washer, who had a burden to continue the church mission. He was retiring, the church was dying, and he felt led to link up with this young guy (me) he had met only once. Pastor Washer shared resources with me and the eleven people who formed the core of Oasis Church at that time and sent us out with the support of several families, some of whom were his own children. Eventually, Ojus closed its doors, giving us the building to sell. This event led to the beginning of Oasis Church and the down payment for our present sanctuary.

Nothing you read in the following pages would have ever happened without Pastor Washer and another selfless pastor, Bud McCord of the West Hollywood church. I will be forever grateful to them for believing in me and supporting me. I have often said that every life changed through Christmas at the Oasis and any outreach of Oasis Church is credited in heaven to those two churches and their pastors.

The very first year of our church's existence, Hurricane Andrew and its powerful category-5 winds had blown through South Dade just thirty miles south of us. Considered the most powerful and damaging storm in American history when it hit in 1992, Hurricane Andrew wiped out miles of subdivisions. Many of the dislocated people moved north to the only place with lots of room to start over, Pembroke Pines.

When the church was about two years old, we were meeting in a theater across from a new mall in the third fastest growing city in the United States at the time. The Pembroke Lakes Mall had just opened to much fanfare, and no one was more excited than I was, knowing it would bring more people to the city, boosting our tax base and providing all kinds of opportunities. The community was growing fast, as it was one of the only two cities in our county that were not built out. The Everglades to the west of us limited any further growth, but we had a lot of room for our church, the new mall, and the Everglades—enough to support another one hundred thousand new residents. We had every reason to be excited about where God had placed us. However, as any pastor knows, simply existing in a growing area does not mean your church will grow. Our growth took hard work, lots of prayer and perspiration, and an amazing calling to the vision and mission God gave us. The changes were overwhelming for a small church that first met in a trailer on a few acres and then moved after one year to a movie theater, where the continual setup and takedown continued for two more years.

Little did I know that moving to the theater was one of the most providential decisions in our history. About a year after moving there, we suddenly found ourselves in a firestorm of controversy.

It was Thanksgiving weekend, and the mall was bustling for Black Friday and the upcoming Christmas season. We were busy as a new church trying to do Christmas in a theater and getting ready for that Sunday's service.

Watching the news, I saw a story about a complaint from some of our Jewish neighbors who lived across the street from our church in a large retirement community of eleven thousand people called Century Village. They had complained about Pembroke Lakes Mall not having a menorah in their mall even though it had traditional Christmas scenes like Santa, Frosty, Christmas trees, and a nativity scene.

The mall executives in Chicago decided to put a menorah in the mall. Good decision. But for some reason I will never understand, they decided to take the nativity down and remove it. Such an overreaction! I felt that the nativity needed to be protected. And if one person's call could get it removed, then perhaps another person's call could get it put back in.

So, I called the mall office and spoke with the public relations manager but made no progress. I then asked to talk with the manager, and my request fell on deaf ears. The decision was final. No Jesus.

Being a stubborn person who feels that keeping with principle and conviction is always better than winning arguments, I did not stop there.

On this particular holiday weekend, the biggest weekend of the year for the retail business, I called for a protest in front of the Pembroke Lakes Mall. I am neither a boycotter nor a protester, and to this day this was the only protest I've ever organized.

On Black Friday, the busiest shopping weekend of the year, our little band of around thirty protesters stood at the main entrance to the mall. We held up signs and waved at the thousands of shoppers who came and went. The signs said, "Put Jesus Back in the Mall," "Put the Menorah and Nativity Side by Side," "Jesus Is the Reason for the Season," and other similar sayings. Moms with babies, small children, and even my own mom showed up to lend a hand. She was the most senior member of Oasis Church and had never been in a protest in her life. It was a sight to see: my sweet little, quiet, shy mom standing on a street corner protesting. Some of the protesters even dressed up as Joseph, Mary, the shepherds, and the wise men.

That day was the catalyst to Christmas at the Oasis. Today, over a million people have driven onto our six acres during these twenty-five days of December. I would have never imagined it starting with a protest about banning Jesus from a mall.

But the events that followed led to our present-day CATO.

The *Miami Herald* and the *Fort Lauderdale Sun-Sentinel* newspapers and the local TV stations covered the protest, which got the attention of the mall's big boys in Chicago. Within a day, they had called us for a face-to-face. Two days later, the executives were in South Florida meeting with us in the mall conference room.

I made it clear we did not want to remove the menorah, Frosty, or even Santa Claus. We acknowledged their place in the traditional Christmas in America. About an hour of contentious discussion ensued. Then the public relations manager said something I'll never forget. It dug deep in my soul. She said, "I don't know what else you guys want. You have Frosty, Santa, and the Christmas tree that represent Christians. What else do you want? Meeting adjourned."

They went back to their plush offices in Chicago while I went back to my tiny little trailer office feeling like a total failure. We had lost and looked like fools outside the mall carrying on with our protest. I remember distinct feelings of disappointment and even anger creeping into my soul that Thanksgiving weekend.

Monday morning came. I arrived at the office, where I had a secretary a few days a week for about four hours a day. All was pretty simple: a dot-matrix printer (also called an impact printer) and an Atari computer. A message was sitting on my desk. On that proverbial pink phone message pad of the past were these words: "Call Father Jim at St. Maximilian Kolbe Catholic Church." What could that possibly be? The only association I had ever had with a Catholic priest or church was when they had sent a potted plant to our little trailer to welcome us to the community on our first Sunday, September 15, 1991. I remember being so appreciative because Baptists and Catholics generally did not mix. And so, with this call, a special friendship began, although short-lived, since Father Jim died about five years later.

When I called Father Jim, he said, "Guy, I've been watching the news about the nativity at the mall. I saw your protest." His church was directly on the east side of the mall. The theater where we met at was on the south side, very close.

He went on to encourage me and let me know he agreed the mall had made a mistake. But he said we should not expect anything else from those who do not know Jesus. Then he lowered the boom on me in his winsome and pleasant way. He said, "I wonder how many churches have the nativity on their lawns? Why would we expect a business whose purpose is to sell and make money to have something even *we* do not have?" He was right. Our little trailer had plenty of land—we had even just bought six acres right out on Flamingo Road, the busiest north-south road in our city.

He proposed we put up *our* nativities and get people to focus on Christmas on *our* land. Father Jim proposed that all the churches get together for a nativity lighting ceremony to show our unity and support of the real reason for Christmas. Then Father Jim got really crazy. He suggested his church would host an outside nativity lighting across from the mall the following Friday night. He wanted us to be there, pray, and join in this ceremony. That was a bridge too far for me, but I listened. I told him I would get back to him. As we ended the call, he said something that makes me laugh to this day: "I know you Baptists and Protestants have a lot of issues with our Roman Catholic faith, and by the way, I do too. But I want to put the nativity not on our land but in the lake on our property. We will float it to the middle and light it there during the ceremony. Then it will not be on "Roman land.""

His statement was so clever and funny at the same time. Father Jim was an exceptional person. We later went on to try putting together a faith-based worship center out in the newest communities where the land was so expensive. All the churches could share it. I will forever be grateful to Father Jim and his call that Monday morning.

The ceremony took place the following Friday. I sent my part-time worship leader and associate to represent us. I had already gone way out of my comfort zone in protesting with the mall executives. But joining a Catholic priest in an interfaith service? I was not ready for that, so I sent my worship leader. It was a cop-out, I know, but I had earned some street credibility from the protest.

That very week, I went to our local Walmart and bought a metal nativity scene, lit it, and put it on the lawn of our trailer. I said I would never again be guilty of not displaying "the reason for the season" or letting our property go dark on Christmas.

And so, Christmas at the Oasis had begun.

Three Hundred Lights and a Nativity

"Go therefore and make disciples of all nations,
baptizing them in the name of the Father
and of the Son and of the Holy Spirit."

—Matthew 28:19

If you are a pastor reading this, or a layperson who wants to pass this along to your pastor as an idea of how to reach your community, let me remind you that a lack of budget, size, location, and even buildings is no reason to delay starting a Christmas outreach.

My part-time worship leader and I put the first lights in the hedge outside our little trailer— three hundred mini-lights we bought from Walmart and the metal nativity. They were enjoyed by our twenty-five volunteers who came to our Christmas party that year. We still display that nativity all these years later. The same hedge is there today and now shines bright with a couple of thousand lights every Christmas. While this first year was not the official beginning of Christmas at the Oasis, it was its birth.

I do not remember the exact time CATO came to me, nor the plan to make it a community celebration and outreach. The seeds had been planted during my phone call with Father Jim.

CATO was a vision to help carry out our mission "to be and to make disciples." But it was not some grand ambition that was totally impossible to achieve.

I had come from a church that did cantatas, large musicals sometimes paired with other theatrics. They were performed each Easter and Christmas. These programs could attract hundreds, and for larger churches, even thousands. They required a very large budget. They also required extensive practice and could involve only people with musical or theatrical talent. For many years, the cantata was a wonderful tool for telling the Easter and Christmas stories. God used it to bring many people to Christ. But few churches use this tool today.

Yes, CATO came out of a protest and call from a priest, but it was a God thing. He planted the seed in my heart, but it was also a move of practicality and common sense.

I realized our church could not afford large theatrical shows, and several large churches were already doing these within miles of us. We could never compete in talent or money to bring in the community. Cantatas usually drew mostly the church members and Christians from other churches. That too bothered me because our church had begun with a distinct purpose: to reach those who were not in church or did not know Jesus. Honestly, our goal wasn't to entertain the church person. That sounds harsh, but it is not our calling. That is why we have never advertised in church magazines, religious papers, or on Christian radio or TV. That is not where Jesus told us to go. He put a burden on our hearts for the lost sheep, and that is why Christmas at the Oasis began and continues today.

The Power of a Story

You've probably heard that the most potent advertising strategy is to share a story. Whether a company is selling a product or a politician is trying to connect with potential voters, real-life stories are effective. In both the secular and the spiritual worlds, the power of a story moves people.

The last thing I would insinuate is that we want to manipulate people to come to church. That is the wrong motivation for doing ministry. To tell a story to manipulate a certain outcome, build attendance, or raise an offering can be alluring; it is very human. Regardless of our end game, the story must be truthful and without guile or selfish motivation. That's a fine line, and sometimes it is hard to know if we've crossed it.

At Oasis Church, we have always told stories, though we have not always done it enough; it's easy to get lazy and not share stories. Why? Because stories take time. Using stories is messy, and no story is final, so we take a risk.

Throughout this book, in sections called "The Power of a Story," I am going to share stories of people affected by Christmas at the Oasis over the years. We will continue to post more stories at Changingyourcommunity.com (more information on page 115).

The work and investment in CATO are not worthwhile if they don't result in life change. Christ's working in hearts at Christmas is the main goal. All the lights, displays, and events are a waste of time if we are just trying to get attention for our church. When we talk about impacting our community, it is with the desire to live out the Great Commission of our Lord, who told us to baptize and disciple. That is the reason we do Christmas—a motive sometimes hard to get across to people, even to a staff member. I've told our church and staff many times that all the work we do for Christmas is not worthwhile unless people's lives are changed and we hear stories of how CATO played a part.

Stop right now and ask God to give you an open mind and heart as you read these stories. Would you want to be involved with something like this? Would you want your church to experience this life-changing holiday? I hope you will. But weigh the cost. I believe most churches will not do this, but not because they do not love God or believe in the Great Commission—all profess that they do. It often boils down to one thing: too much work. Most would not say it aloud, but I do think many churches are not willing to take on so much work.

To me, the stories on the following pages make everything we have done during Christmas worthwhile.

I have shared my story about how I fell in love with Christmas and how Christmas at the Oasis began. Now I want to share stories from our staff. I asked them to share their stories as I prepared this book and will sprinkle them throughout the chapters.

Why staff? There are so many stories, it's hard to keep track of them. Honestly, I have not done well keeping them in files over the years. But these stories come straight from those who lead and make CATO work. I am no longer the driving force behind this massive local church endeavor we call Christmas at the Oasis. It outgrew me many years ago. I could lead it, but I couldn't pastor, preach, and carry out my other roles as senior pastor if I did. I am grateful to those who over the years have picked up the mantle of Christmas, impacting our community. We would not still be doing it if it were not for their unselfish giving of time, resources, and gifts.

This is the most crucial part of introducing the stories: all but a few of these staff members, whose time with us ranges from a few years to more than twenty, came from within Oasis Church. They were not recruited. For the most part, they came to Oasis as "normal" people, I like to say. This fact makes their stories even more compelling and unique. They loved Oasis before they "worked" here. You will see in their stories that some of them even came to Oasis because of the Christmas display.

Take my assistant, Katia, and her family, for instance. Their story grips me no matter how many times I hear it. Katia is also the one who edits my books and works with other editors, printers, and graphic artists. She has made it easier to publish this third book. I am glad God led her and her family here. You will read her story later in the next chapter. Some of our team members will also share touching stories they witnessed during this past year.

I often say the ones who get the most out of CATO are the ones who serve. They are on the front lines as they see lives changed, families united, and, ultimately, people coming to Christ and being baptized. You will catch a glimpse of all this as they recount their memories.

THE POWER OF A STORY

For the One
From: John Falco, Production Experience Director

John is one of the smartest young men I have ever known. His own family came to our church when he was just a little kid. We met them while staying on Hollywood Beach some twenty years ago. It was a God thing. John possesses a unique perspective because he has been here since he was little. He now oversees the most complex part of CATO, the light wall that encircles much of the main auditorium and is sequenced to do music and light shows continually throughout December. You just have to see it to appreciate it. It is breathtaking. —PG

Growing up in Oasis, I have seen many different phases of CATO. Most notably, early on in my childhood, going to CATO became a family tradition. Whether we were attending church regularly or not, CATO was always a huge part of our Christmas celebrations. I also remember being up in Nashville for the Light-o-Rama Conference (software used to run the wall of lights) training and meeting a gentleman who had heard I was from Oasis in South Florida. He came up to me so excited to meet me. He told me he and his family take an annual drive from North Carolina to South Florida and back during the holidays. They make an effort to catch about a dozen different light displays throughout the southeast. He mentioned that Oasis was always one of their last stops since we are so far south, and he was so thankful that our display was part of such a huge family tradition for them also.

Now that is making an impact far beyond your community. It might be a little more than you can envision right now, but you catch the impact: not just the way it impacted a family who made CATO one of their Christmas traditions, but also the way it impacted John as a child (he now oversees a vital portion of it). That is a great reason for starting your display

or serving in your Christmas outreach right there. Here's the
conclusion of John's story. —PG

"One person at a time" is a big saying at Oasis. We might touch thousands, but Jesus touched one person at a time. He spoke and taught to thousands, but that *one* was who He came at Christmas for and died for at Easter. One person. Our focus is always on the *one*. We must remind ourselves of this all the time, especially at Christmas, when up to five thousand people come some nights—although we try to limit the numbers because of safety concerns and our small property. Mine is simply another story about the *one*.

Uber, Coast Guard, and Cancer
From: Alex Rivera, Executive Pastor

At the time this book is being written, Alex and his wife,
Arelis, have been with us for seven years. Alex heard of
Oasis in college from another pastor when he was moving back
to South Florida. I will never forget the morning he showed
up out of nowhere to volunteer for our worship band. From
there, he began to serve regularly on our worship team. We
saw something special in him and hired him part-time, which
eventually grew to full-time. Today he is one of our pastors.
He and Arelis were married here; Arelis also served as a
volunteer and later served as our Oasis Kids Director and
staff person for our Missions Team. This couple is special.
We are blessed to have them on our team. —PG

Uber

One day after work, I had to take an Uber home. It had been a long day and long week in the middle of Christmas at the Oasis and preparations for Christmas services. On the ride home, the driver was quiet. I didn't mind; I was tired and didn't feel like engaging in small talk. However, halfway through the ride, I felt I had to say something to him. I asked him how long he had been driving. He said he drove full time and reciprocated by asking what I did. I told him I'm a pastor at the church where he had just picked me up. I asked him if he had ever attended. He smiled and said, "I go every year. I love your light display." He shared that he had been taking his daughter and wife for the past couple of years, ever since they came from Venezuela. It had been a time for him to enjoy some time with the family since finances were tight for them, and they often didn't have the money to go out. He even had a few suggestions for us and wanted to let us know he was blessed by Christmas at the Oasis.

Coast Guard

One Sunday during the Christmas season on a weekend I was teaching, I challenged our church to serve. After the service, a couple of young adults came up to me in the lobby and asked if they could serve that night. I said sure, I was serving that night too. I honestly didn't think they would show up, but I was pleasantly surprised when they did. We talked and got to know each other as we served together.

Both were in the U.S. Coast Guard and stationed in Miami. They had found Oasis Church and began attending consistently. They were with us their entire time in South Florida until they were transferred somewhere else. They would even bring the family to church from Rhode Island and Puerto Rico when they came to town.

Cancer

One day in the lobby, I was greeted by a first-time guest. She was joining us for a weekend service. Her best friend had just died, and her granddaughter had just been diagnosed with cancer. I remember her saying, "This is my first time coming. I came last week with my family to see the lights, and when I got the news, I didn't know where else to go." I was able to pray with her. She had learned of us through CATO and was able to find a place to grieve when she had no other place to go.

Oasis Church is one of the most diverse churches in America. Members have emigrated from over ninety countries. Many are just beginning to speak English and learning about American culture. Oasis has been a wonderful place for them. People from many places and walks of life live in South Florida. It is such a blessing to be family for the military families; Christmas is a great catalyst to connect them. Then there are the families that come with heavy burdens, and we pray for them, love them, and help bring some sunshine and joy into their lives at Christmas.
—PG

Dream = Excitement = Fail = Catastrophe

The LORD upholds all who fall and
lifts up all who are bowed down.

—*Psalm 145:14*

Just because you have a dream does not mean you will not experience any failures. Even when exercising faith, there is a chance of failure. I believe the greater the faith, the greater the opportunity to fail. We would not call it faith if the outcome were assured. One of my dreams we tried at Oasis at Christmas became our greatest failure and almost cost me my ministry.

Early on in this journey, the sky was the limit. It was not a matter of asking ourselves, did we have the funds, volunteers, and staff to pull it off? What we *did* have were big dreams. It quickly became evident to me that what had started as controversy had become a great way for us to impact our community.

Our beginnings appear small and insignificant to anyone outside our original six acres of sawgrass, which is swamp—the Everglades.

Dreams cost nothing, and boy did I have dreams! The more I dreamed, the more they kept coming. To this day, I do not share most of my ideas and dreams for Christmas at the Oasis or even Oasis Church since so many people cannot handle them. The magnitude would scare them to death. I do not want to lose all my staff, so most of my dreams I have kept between God and me. I then slowly share them with those closest at first. The proverbial trial balloon, as they say. A little secret is that I do not say this is a dream or a vision. I mention it only in passing as an idea and see how it lands. Most of the time, it is met with a laugh or someone saying it would never work. But I do not let someone else's lack of vision keep me from mine—and you shouldn't either. Still, vocalizing it helps me start to flesh it out and hear how it sounds outside my brain.

Over the years, dreams have not stopped coming. But I will tell you that everything we do on only six acres becomes more challenging with time. That is good news for someone reading this and contemplating reaching thousands in your community, but you may not know where to start. I am coming to that in the later chapters.

I have heard it said that one thing we have learned from history is that we do not learn from history. I would say one of the best things I've done in my more than four decades of full-time ministry is to try to learn from others. I do not consider myself unusually creative or a great person of faith. What I have tried to do is learn from others, from their successes and their failures.

I hope our greatest failure will also be a good lesson to those who may be contemplating their own Christmas outreach.

Oasis continued to grow as a young, baby church. Along with our attendance growth came the growth of Christmas at the Oasis. That progress was exciting and challenging. We had only six acres of land

and one little trailer. That first small trailer was soon joined by a triple-wide, which is still used today as our Christmas work trailer, along with housing other offices.

Because of the cost of land in South Florida, we do not have large and sprawling campuses. We sit on only six acres of land, and almost a third of that is mandated for water retention. We have always done what it takes on such a limited space. It is South Florida, and as they say, they aren't making any more land. Regardless of our limitations, we have found a way to expand CATO over the last twenty-five years and bring up to fifty-two thousand people onto the property each Christmas. How? We will discuss that later in the book. But if you are a church with lots of land, you can do Christmas even better than we do and have a much larger canvas to paint on. If you are a small church with only an acre of land or a church plant with no land, yes, you can do this same Christmas outreach.

I heartily believe any church can do this!

But what about failure? We all like to hear stories of failures even though we might not say so aloud. Well, we have had our share of failures, but this one is the most painful to me. I have only shared it a few times with our congregation, so many do not know the story. But they will now.

The most famous attraction in South Florida is our beaches. People come by the millions each year to visit them. But there are prettier ones elsewhere in the state, such as the Florida panhandle beaches, which are often voted the most beautiful in the world.

Why are our beaches so famous? The weather! When it snows in other areas of the country and cabin fever hits its fever pitch, we are basking in eighty-degree weather. If you live in the north, you know what I mean. That was the perfect setup for our greatest failure.

I love snow and try to visit the north at least once each winter. Most of our staff planning retreats are held in the north in January and February so we can experience the beauty of snow and the nip of the frosty air. It also helps put us in the mood to evaluate the past Christmas and begin planning for the following one. Our groundwork requires year-round planning and effort.

Growing up in South Florida, I did not see snow until I was in college. I never had a fireplace and never skied.

Over the years in South Florida, I have seen cities and other large gatherings that would re-create the north and bring in "snow"—ice shredded up and blown over the ground into a big hump. For a small price, the kids get ten minutes to throw the snow, roll in the snow, and act as if they are up north. They even dress in their winter clothes if they have some. These snow events have always been popular in South Florida during Christmas. I dreamed of adding such an event to CATO one day.

My dream was about to become a reality.

In our third year of the Christmas drive-through, we tried something *big*. The first couple of years, our display started with a drive-through. No one got out of the car. They just drove through the property and looked at the light displays. The light displays that have been a big part of our three decades are essentially a piece of metal molded into a figure with lights strung on it. It can be a snowman, word, or any other form you can dream up. The drive-through experience is still a significant part of CATO even today, but not all events and displays are used annually. Some have been retired for various reasons, and some happen only once because they failed or, in this case, were a disaster.

I decided it was time to get people out of their cars. The first goal of our drive-through was to get people to drive onto the church property. Do you know how hard it is to get nonchurch people to visit one? Simply getting them on the property would be a big win. That was our first goal as a new church with only a trailer. We needed to be in sight. You could drive by fifty miles per hour and never even know a church was there. The lights in trees and bushes were a small but important step. People notice lights, especially at Christmas. After we began to draw several thousand people to the property to drive through, I wanted to take it a step further.

Let's get them out of their cars to smell the air, meet a few of our church family members, and see we're normal people like them. We began with several things.

Because our culture is so diverse, we had begun to attract people from other regions, especially the Caribbean. The first year or two we hired a steel band and advertised opening night. We wanted to have a grand opening to kick off our month of Christmas. We did this for several years until the crowds outgrew the property and parking. I wish we could still do it; the anticipation of turning on the lights all at once is still something with lots of memories. Along with the steel band, we wanted something to attract the families. Snow was the answer.

Opening night for Lighting Up the Pines had arrived, and the anticipation was as high as I had ever seen on our property. One of my dreams had become a reality.

We were going to have "real snow" in South Florida! We advertised in the local papers and sent press releases to radio, TV, and other media. The Miami Herald sent a reporter to do a feature story for the Southwest Broward edition of the Sunday paper. It was the perfect setting for our first opening night when people got out of the cars. We did not sell tickets. We just rented the snow machine and went with it.

This little church of two-hundred people was prepared, or so we thought. And then it happened. One thousand people showed up for the snow. I had envisioned one thousand people at the beginning of this new church, filling up the church along with the eleven original founding members. And now, this. Success!

This was five times more people than we had ever had on our property. What a night it was going to be.

The steel band was playing Caribbean Christmas music. People were excited and could not wait to unleash their kids onto the snow. There was only one problem: the snow machine was not there. The ropes were up, volunteers staged, lines formed, but no snow. On a simple bullhorn, we implored the crowd to be patient. All the while, I grew nervous. What if the snow guy doesn't show? We had spent a good amount of money for this, and that was weighing on my mind too.

He was forty-five minutes late, but he finally arrived. Christmas was saved, and we had averted an embarrassing disaster. A huge vehicle the size of a garbage truck lumbered in with a strange machine called a snowmaker. The driver climbed out, and, with no apology or reason for his tardiness, began to do his thing.

Success? Well, yes and no.

The snow machine began to do its job, but something in the driver's head went off when he saw all those excited kids. With a large black hose the size of a sewer pipe, he began to blow the snow all over the crowd. The crowd went into a frenzy. The lines we had developed became nonexistent. The more snow he blew onto the crowd, the more out of control it became, and the more he played to the audience.

Finally, a snow hill began to form, but the excited crowd had become a mob and was totally out of control. All semblance of order was gone.

Kids began to play King of the Mountain on the snow, shoving and pushing. One crazy kid began to take this ice we called snow and make snowballs. The ice was not like the soft-packed snow from the north, but more like ice cubes. These solid weapons used against another person could be dangerous.

At this point, the bullhorn didn't work; it could not be heard over the chaos. The few policemen in our church and a local fire captain took matters into their own hands. They began to get kids off the hill and scream at parents. By now kids were hit and hurt. One mother screamed that her child had been hit in the eye and was bleeding.

I did what every good pastor would do at a time like this—I walked away. Yes, I walked away. During the chaos and rioting, I left. I had no idea what to do. I could just see the lawsuits being filed and the *Miami Herald* front page reading, "Riot at Pembroke Pines Church Injures 150 Children."

With no idea of what to do, I left it in the hands of the cops and the fireman. I walked to the other end of the dark property out by the highway. It was only sawgrass at the time, and it became my sanctuary that night in the swamp. I walked and prayed. I was fearful, in shock, and discouraged. I saw no good ending to this. To me, this turn of events was the end of Christmas in the Pines, the end of this new growing church, and the end of my pastorate. The cops and the fireman finally got the crowd under control and back in somewhat of an orderly line. But the night had been chaos and a total failure.

I went home that night discouraged. It's the only time in our thirty-year history that I have wanted to quit. I tried to picture how I would do it. Should I resign on Sunday morning and apologize? Or should

I wait until the lawsuits and the *Miami Herald* article came out and the church rose against me? It was a terrible night, and I slept very little.

Sunday morning came, but I did not want to get up. The only thing that motivated me to get out of the house was that I needed to read the *Miami Herald* article about this disaster. I quickly got dressed and drove to the closest 7-11 and bought a Sunday newspaper. I immediately went to the Broward section. Sure enough, on the front page was our church.

What was not in the picture or the article was anything about the disaster. By God's grace, the reporter ignored the negative and told the story of the night just as I had dreamed it to be months earlier. I wish I knew who she was; I would probably buy her a new house because she saved my ministry with that one article. There's never been a more positive story written about our church.

We have never had another snow hill. Sometimes in a planning meeting a new staff member will bring up the idea of real snow. They are promptly told "not under my watch."

We survived. There were no lawsuits or hospital bills. Other failures would follow over the years, but none so bad as this one.

THE POWER OF A STORY

From Ecuador, with Love and a Skeptical Husband
From: Katia Droira, Senior Pastor's Assistant

Katia and her husband have a beautiful story of how they came to Oasis. As you have read from others, many of their journeys began during a Christmas display they visited one year. Katia is no different. She and her family are also immigrants who bring a rich and beautiful culture to our church. Katia is one of the most loving, godly people I know. I am honored to serve with her and to be on this journey with her and her family. I like to say I may be the only pastor in America with an editor who speaks English as a second language and who makes my English presentable. She is incredible, but her story and heart are even more so. —PG

The smiles were beaming, kindness in their eyes shining as bright as the lights we had come to see. We had arrived at Christmas at the Oasis in Pembroke Pines. We were new to South Florida— we had moved only a few months before—and this was on our list of places to visit in this new town we would come to love. Little did I know then that Oasis would become an important part of our lives. But before I tell you how our first visit went, let me tell you about the journey that led us to Oasis that Christmas night in 2001.

I had come to trust in Christ Jesus as my Lord and my Savior a year after my dad passed away. I was married and living in the U.S., and my mom and sisters were back in the town in Ecuador where I had grown up. I was grieving but learning about the living God who, in His mercy, gave us eyes to see His love and comfort through a dark season. We were unaware that God was reeling us in one by one. During my dad's illness, I had begun reading God's Word for the first time in my life. I also had started listening to a local Christian radio station almost daily, and my life had begun to change. What would be the odds that a year later as I traveled to Ecuador to celebrate the traditional first-year mass of my dad's passing, my mom, sisters, and I would share with unspeakable joy what God had been doing in our lives? My sisters took me to a Christian church they were already attending. There, I finally and openly surrendered my life to Christ. The Bible speaks about rejoicing in heaven when a sinner repents and is born again in spirit (Luke 15:10). The picture I have of my sisters rejoicing with me that day gives me a glimpse of what that must be like.

This life-changing event led me to a couple of years of prayer, asking God for a church to call home. I wanted so badly to take part in the fellowship of His church. I was reading in His Word of His marvelous design—the God family. My mom and sisters were already partaking in it far away. Many prayers went up for my husband, Jose, to desire a church as I did and for us to find the right one. One day, he finally said, "Okay, we can try finding one, but we both need to agree it's the right one for us." I was jumping with joy and excitement inside.

The following months took us to a whole list of places of worship in our area, but we couldn't agree on one. I continued praying. That is, until the move to South Florida. And here we were, about to tour Christmas at the Oasis when a beautiful volunteer welcomed us. To say that Jose was a little skeptical is an understatement. He said, "Let's get the wallet out because this surely cannot be free! There is nothing free in this life." But they did not ask for money. We drove around, enjoyed the light displays, and even got out of the car to stroll at our leisure. We were impressed; we had not seen anything like it. We had seen Christmas lights before, but in an unexplainable way, this was different—and all done with love.

We were about to leave when a volunteer, placed "strategically" at the exit, approached us. Jose quickly said, "See, what did I tell you? It was too good to be true." Reaching for his wallet, he said, "Nothing is free." He rolled the window down and held out some bills in his hand. The kind lady said, "Oh, no! We don't accept donations! All this is for you and your family. We hope you had a great time!" Jose was speechless. We both were. Not only did she refuse the money, but she also gave us all candy canes to enjoy on our way home, the gesture representing in a very simple way gospel love, free and unconditional.

Jose was so moved, and I was fighting back tears. Had God heard my prayers? I had spent over two years looking and waiting for that church that felt like home. That night, I heard Jose say, "This church is different. Let's go to their service on Sunday."

God chose Oasis to be part of our training ground to love and be loved as He does and to be part of the family of God.

Jose is no longer a skeptic. He has been a deacon, lay pastor, and Spanish interpreter for our services, assisting in our Spanish service. He serves anywhere and everywhere. He and Katia are two of the people who make Oasis a very special place. I love them as friends and fellow members. I am so glad God led them here through Christmas at the Oasis. —PG

Impacting Your Community in 25 Days

And let us consider how to stir up one
another to love and good works.

—*Hebrews 10:24 ESV*

Up to now, you've read our church's story and the backstory of Christmas at the Oasis. Now I want to share how CATO has positively impacted our community for over twenty-five years and encourage you that you can impact your community as well. Today, thousands come, and many make it a yearly tradition. We are known throughout the South Broward community as the Christmas church.

Pastors are often known to ask, "If your church were to shut down today, would anyone notice or even care?" May I ask you that question right now? If your church shut down today, would anyone other than your members notice? Would the community even care? What has your church done in your community that people would miss? That question used to haunt me. For many years, I wondered if no one would notice other than our members.

Our city has 180,000 residents. A neighboring city has over 160,000. Several others north of us have another 100,000 each. And east of us is the hometown I grew up in, Hollywood, with over 160,000. That's a lot of people. Our county has over 1.5 million, Dade County over 2.5 million. How in the world do you impact that many people? When you think of those numbers, the challenge is formidable. To think that 96 percent of them are not professing Christians, one of the highest percentages in the United States, then it is simply overwhelming.

You might be on the opposite side of this coin. If you live in a rural area, your town may number in the hundreds, and you may think you are too small to make an impact. Perhaps you feel that everyone has a church already. Regardless of your issues, that focus is wrong.

First, as the church, we have the mission Jesus gave us two thousand years ago: go, teach, and baptize. Our church has interpreted the Great Commission of Matthew 28:18–20 this way: "be and make disciples." Almost every church would agree that this is the church's mission. Most churches would also say they are working toward it and believe in it. However, most of those same churches have not found a way to expand that mission in their city or neighborhood. Many are frustrated by the culture, the direction of our nation, and the little difference the church seems to be making. I share that frustration and concern. It weighs on me daily, and it's likely most pastors share that concern.

There are many ways to impact a community and live out the Great Commission. Thousands of books have been written on ways to do it. Many of them are good, but some just rehash what's been said and done for decades. For this reason, I resisted writing this book for many years.

I finally decided we have a way and a road less traveled that *any church* can take to impact a community in twenty-five days. Few resources like this are available to help churches tackle mass evangelism and impact a community.

We still reach people one person at a time. That is a mantra I remind our staff and church of constantly. But let's face it, we all want to reach as many as we can because God tells us to and because people's coming to Jesus saves them from the grips of hell. That's direct, I know. But if that is not why we do what we do, then we need to shut down and go do something else.

Most large outreaches can be done only by large churches with thousands of members. That keeps many on the sidelines when it comes to community impact. If we are honest, many of us are just trying to figure out how to keep our churches together following the coronavirus pandemic of 2020.

The final straw that made me write this book was COVID-19. During the pandemic, we had little idea of what things would look like when we got back to "normal." But I suggest we will never get back to normal. Since COVID-19, things are proving to be very different. Most in-house congregations are smaller. For many, reaching people is more difficult than ever, and finances are being stretched.

So why challenge churches to spend more money and do more outreach with fewer volunteers? Because I know something I want to share with you.

The issues the pandemic has created do not stop us from doing Christmas the way we have for years. Our Christmas outreach enables us to reach people without requiring them to enter the buildings. If you follow the guidelines we've used at Oasis Church, you'll find it is a cost-effective outreach.

It would be a mistake to focus on the thousands we reach and the size of our budget for Christmas. The good news is, no matter the size of your budget or membership, you can impact your community in just twenty-five days. This approach has worked for us and, best of all, it is not rocket science.

I have already shared how CATO began with one lit metal nativity and three hundred lights. Each year our goal was to add a little more. I found a place to buy metal Christmas displays at wholesale. We would put our lights on the metal displays of trees, reindeer, snowmen, and people figures. Then it was just a matter of where to place the figures.

People began to notice the lights. At first, they would drive through. But as we began to organize, we advertised in various ways, much of it through free public service announcements. Before long, we had several thousand people driving through our property. That figure grew each year until its peak of fifty-two thousand around 2008. Our lack of land keeps us from expanding much beyond that, but God in His faithfulness gives us plenty of prospects each year.

Focus on your neighborhood, people, building, and land. What could you do to begin? Could you put some lights on your buildings? Could you put lights on your trees? Do you have someone who could build wooden displays and light them? The potential is endless, yet it takes little to get started. I'm not suggesting starting with a half-million lights like we have today or spending $100,000 as we now do each year. A few hundred dollars will get you started. Later in the book, we'll look at how you can raise money without taking it from your budget.

You may ask how a thousand lights and a few lit trees could impact your community. Look around. What other church puts up lights? You may be surprised at how few even have a nativity on their lawn.

Just putting lights up gets attention and sets you apart. That's a start. It may not bring a lot of families at first, but people will begin to notice.

We often say in our church that ministry is a journey, not a sprint. It could similarly be said, a Christmas outreach is a journey, not a sprint. You build on what you did the year before. You do not look at each year as a journey in itself. Longevity is your best friend if you want to impact your community in the twenty-five days from December 1 to December 25. Twenty-five days may turn into twenty-five years, or even twenty-five thousand people visiting your church annually at Christmas.

I believe that with all my heart. When God called me to plant Oasis, I prayed He would let me stay here the rest of my life. As of this writing, we are in our thirty-first year. I don't know what tomorrow will bring, but I do know He's been faithful.

The awesome thing about CATO is that we do not have to reinvent the wheel every time. We only tighten some spokes, shine them up, and maybe tweak or add a few more. Many churches feel the pressure every Easter and Christmas to come up with a new plan. We still do that at Easter, but at Christmas, we go back, evaluate, pray, dream, brainstorm, and build on what we already have. Some of our displays are the original ones.

Christmas is a time for tradition. Bringing things back year after year cultivates tradition. Your church could be one where people engage and build family traditions.

THE POWER OF A STORY

The Little Boy and the Train
From: Mayra Saintilus, Former Oasis Kids' Ministry Staff

Mayra grew up at Oasis and went through all our youth ministries. Now a young adult, Mayra has become one of our key leaders. I love her bubbly personality and the way she loves our kids. We are so honored to see our kids as adult leaders take part as Oasis staff. Our kids' ministry team leads the Christmas train rides, and here, Mayra shares one of their stories. —PG

While working the train station, I noticed a little boy no more than four who was super shy to step up. While standing in the line, I try to play a game to keep the kids busy. This little boy was with his single mom, who was trying to have a good Christmas with her son. I started playing the color guessing game with him, pointing out some lights, our shirts, and all the different colors that surrounded us. After a few rounds, he broke out of his shell and seemed more comfortable. Then they went on their train ride! This family was one of the last families of the night before closing time. When they came back around on the train, the little kid was ecstatic and begged his mom to go again, but she did not have any more tickets. The volunteer helping people on and off the train saw that there were only two families for the last train ride. She asked me if it was all right for them to go again. Of course, they rode again. After their last ride, the mother came up to me and the volunteer and thanked us for such an amazing experience from the whole church. They had not been regular attenders, but at one service when the mom heard our team share about kids' CATO experiences and how so many had been impacted, she seemed appreciative. The next Sunday they showed up, and the boy attended our kids' class while his mom was in service.

Do you see a thread here? Not only does almost every story result in a changed life, but most of the people end up visiting Oasis Church, and many stay. Some make it a holiday thing, but I am glad they come then at least. At any moment, God can work in their lives to make them fully devoted followers of Christ. —PG

From Volunteer to Cancer to the Next Generation
From: Marsha Lowe, Community Groups Director

Marsha and her husband, Garfield, and their wonderful daughter, Samantha, have been a part of Oasis for many years. Like most of those telling their stories, they started as volunteers and now are key leaders, with Garfield being our pastoral care pastor. Marsha has led our community ministries with small groups for all ages, in all places, studying the Bible and living in community. Dr. Lowe, as you may hear people call her, is a wonderful person. Along with her intelligence, she has an unforgettable smile. She is such a joy to serve with and brings so much to our church family. Even though she has earned a doctorate in organizational leadership and human services administration, she chose to serve on our team during this season of life, earning far less money and with a title far less prestigious than she would as a university professor or administrator. Get ready. This story is a tearjerker in several ways. (Note our next generation is already leading during CATO.) —PG

I thought I would share my Christmas at the Oasis story. I say *story* because over the years it has become part of my life story.

My earliest memory of Christmas at the Oasis is as a volunteer, but it has been so long ago I can't remember the exact year. I saw all the hard work that went into it, but actually seeing the full display blew my mind. I had experienced other walk-through Christmas displays but nothing like CATO. There's just palpable energy that permeates the property. You get excited and feel a sense of awe when you hear people gasp in wonder at the lights. It is so exciting when they talk to others about their must-do annual family tradition of visiting CATO and about how much they look forward to visiting even if they've moved out of town. I also saw it through my little girl's eyes. She must have been four or five at the time, which means it was almost two decades ago. I still have a picture of her "driving" the fake Zamboni with Pastor Pat pushing her around the skating rink. But seeing how excited she was to be a wise man in the live nativity, seeing her start to take in the true meaning of Christmas, that was the start for me. Over the years, I've had the pleasure of seeing many people thank us for offering this glimmer of hope, a light that shines bright in the darkness.

In 2012 when I was diagnosed with cancer, I remember CATO being my light. I was diagnosed in October 2012, and I wasn't working. I was just home by myself with my thoughts, which can be a very dangerous thing. It was in those quiet moments that the what-ifs became monsters I couldn't seem to get away from. I remember Garfield, my husband, had to paint a red brick road in the parking lot for CATO, and he asked me to help him. I suspect it was to get me out of the house, but it could be that he really just needed help. But helping with the painting and serving in other ways helped me live beyond my thoughts. As corny as it may sound, serving at CATO became one of my saving graces in a time when I desperately needed help.

Fast forward some more years to CATO 2019 when my daughter was asked to play one of the main roles in the Oasis Kids' Jingle Jam play. I must point out that being a part of the CATO reenactments over the years had undoubtedly helped her develop her confidence. In 2019, however, I think she truly understood why we do Christmas at the Oasis. On a weekend after one of her performances, she was serving outside in our Oasis Kids' welcoming ministry when a Spanish-speaking family came up to her and started talking. When their comments were translated for her, she shed a tear. She said they told her she was the reason they decided to visit a service at Oasis because they had enjoyed her performance so much.

CATO has undoubtedly had a huge impact in the community. People who were just visiting have gone to the volunteer station while I was serving there to offer to volunteer because they enjoyed CATO so much. CATO is more than an event—it's an act of love.

CATO is not just an event. It is not just crowds of people. It is one person at a time being touched with the love of Jesus on our little corner of the world we call Oasis. I love how our teenagers own CATO. They are a huge part of this ministry, and we could not do it without them. The energy alone they create on the property is amazing. I was a youth pastor for ten years in a large church with hundreds of teens, and I will tell you, I have never seen a church embrace its teens like Oasis does or the teens embrace ministry as our teens do. Samantha is just one example of many young disciples of Christ. —PG

The Most Unlikely Outreach

She wrapped him in cloths and placed him in a manger.

—Luke 2:7

The most unlikely outreach we have done to date resulted in our first Guinness World Record. It started when one of our members brought a manila envelope packed with things she wanted to show me. We were only a few years old as a church and had just begun to put up lights outside. While vacationing, Martha Cook and her husband, Wayne, some of our early members whom I had known my whole life, saw something a church in California did at Christmastime that they thought Oasis should consider. Martha set up a meeting with me and laid it out. I can't say it did much for me. When she told me where she got it, I wanted to nix the idea, but for some reason I did not. I listened and told her I would look it over, pray about it, and consider it.

Martha and Wayne had been visiting their friends in California and went to a Christmas crèche display. A crèche is a nativity. These displays are traditional even in homes that are not religious.

The word *crèche* is French for a crib or the trough that animals eat from. In earlier translations of the Bible and culture, that term was *cratch, cracche, crache, and crècche*. There's a wonderful opportunity in this ancient picture of the birth of Christ.

When Oasis Church started, we called ourselves a contemporary, seeker-friendly church, which was popular in the 1990s. We would still be that today, but we rarely use those words. We are very much grounded in the historic doctrines of the Christian faith. We are a Baptist church, although few people would recognize us as Baptist. We like to say we are Baptist in doctrine and polity but nondenominational in worship and mission.

Because of our nontraditional style of worship and ministry, we have prided ourselves in not being bound by traditions. This is why we've been able to reach our South Florida unchurched and diverse community. This makes ministry more exciting and allows for more innovation.

As a young church, we celebrated our lack of traditions that could be a barrier holding someone back from trying out our church. So, we were a nontraditional church. If we were to incorporate Martha's suggestion, we would be using a traditional Christmas symbol, one dating back two thousand years from an Eastern culture most of us cannot understand.

This was the bias I had toward her request that day back in 1995. I looked through the packet of brochures and details of what she described as this amazing crèche display her friend's church had. She also included pictures of the church's fellowship hall with tables displaying various crèches from their members. Each year the members of the church would loan out their crèches for a few weeks so the local community could come and view them.

This sounded like the most boring, old-fashioned, and outdated thing you could ever do. It was not for Oasis Church in South Florida trying to reach a younger unchurched generation and community. It just did not fit us.

I still had to answer Martha. The real obstacle for me was the name of the church that housed this display. This church we were about to model our first Christmas outreach after was a Mormon church. This was a hurdle. How could a Mormon church that questions the deity of Christ and has so many doctrines that are incompatible with Christianity be doing a crèche display? How could I model our greatest outreach after what a Mormon church was doing? But we did, and I'm glad we did. I learned a long time ago we can learn from all types of churches and people. I've laughed many times when telling people we copied a Mormon church.

We launched our first crèche displays with about seventy nativity scenes we had borrowed from our members. We set them up just as the Mormons did, on church tables, and we advertised the display to our church and community. And they came, a few hundred the first year.

We learned quickly the word *creche* was not understood by most people, so we called it a nativity display after a year or so. We began to do this each year during our light display. Oasis members began to buy nativities when they went on vacation or traveled, and many of us accumulated dozens of nativities that we loaned to the church for a couple of weeks each December. My wife and I still have around forty in our attic.

During a sabbatical, the thought of being a part of the Guinness World Record seemed to just pop into my mind, and we set about to reach that goal—eventually, we actually set two records: **crèches** and later the most live lit trees in one location, forever a reminder of our Trees of Hope outreach. The year we set the world record for the largest crèche display, one person lent us a hundred of hers. One of our members had told her about our display and that we were trying to break the record. We were blessed to have them in our record-breaking year before she moved away.

So, if you are not sure you want to go all-in on a light display, you can do the nativity display, with virtually no cost. You can borrow other people's displays and put them on tables you already use in your church and, if need be, borrow tables from other churches.

As our display grew, guests began to lend us their displays, and that created even greater outreach to those who were not part of our church.

For many years we have had up to twelve thousand people come through our auditorium just to see the nativity display. Most of these were not from our church. Being in an area with a large Catholic population, we learned this was a big draw. It is not unusual to see a person crossing themselves while kneeling at our altar and weeping at the sight of so many nativities that remind them of their precious Lord's birth. For many, it's a very holy experience. Most visitors have no idea what type of church we are, and that is probably the number one question we get from visitors at Christmas.

I doubt you have seen guests kneeling at your altar and weeping, but we have. It's so moving. God gave us this unlikely way to touch our community with the supernatural story of salvation.

THE POWER OF A STORY

My Best CATO Memory
From: Justine Cohen, Church Council Member and Volunteer Leader

Justine is one of the hundreds of volunteers who serve during Christmas at the Oasis. She does not serve on our staff; she is a CPA and serves on our church council. With them, she oversees our budgets as well as other strategic ministries. —PG

My best memory of Christmas at the Oasis is the first time CATO did the snow village, and I had the job of turning the snow on and off. The sheer joy on the kids' faces made my night. I ended up turning it on more than needed, just so the kids could stay happy.

Now don't confuse the snow debacle with the snow blowers. We do have snow, but it is not cold, and it is not ice. It does create memories and a lot of amazing smiles from the kids. It is one of the most effective things we do and yet it costs very little with a high return. —PG

Longevity Builds Credibility
From Nikki Sonko, Young Adult Leader and Former Church Council Member

Nikki may have the most infectious smile at Oasis and possesses a heart of gold to go with it. I don't know of any other person at Oasis who exemplifies our motto, "Be the Drop," as much as Nikki does. She is not on our staff but has served on our church council. She also leads our Oasis Young Adults ministry. I love her so much. Nikki loves everyone she meets, and they love her. She's just one of those people. —PG

My best memory is living at the St. Andrews apartment complex across the street from Oasis Church and always seeing the lights when I was growing up, to the point that I always looked forward to seeing them every year. It doesn't really mean it's the Christmas season until I see the lights at the church.

Nikki is one of the hundreds who eventually come to CATO for a church service. That is why it is important to do whatever you do every year. Longevity builds credibility, and it also allows you to see seeds that have been scattered, watered, and prepared for many years begin to sprout. Nikki is a beautiful example of this. —PG

But God . . .
From: Alexis Robinson, Former Oasis Staff

Alexis is one of the most creative people I have ever met. God has blessed us with so many people over the years, but none as creative as Alexis. Training the next generation and the next one after that is her heart. This is a different take on stories yet just as important to the discipleship of believers as young as six or seven years old. I am thankful for those giving their lives using their gifts to teach and train our young children. Alexis served several years with our Oasis Kids ministry, and she talks about children performing a live play during CATO. —PG

I'm someone who always loved performing, but last year I wanted to challenge myself and felt challenged by God to write our CATO show. I was flustered, frustrated, and contemplated just re-doing what had been done the past few years. But God gave me the words and the cast, and He provided the lives to touch. I saw God at work in so many ways that season, but one of the most beautiful moments was witnessing the reactions of our audience. There were children actively engaged and chuckles from parents and random passersby. One of the most delightful God moments was having people come up and ask to talk to the actors.

To see God honor the work and dedication of these volunteers, so many of whom had stepped out of their comfort zone, was humbling for me. I witnessed anointing coming to light and people walking into purpose—kids and adults alike. I know that God planted seeds of hope and things to consider into individuals during that season, and it is a blessing to know that it happened to both strangers and friends.

Another thread that runs through almost every story is the words **hope, love, light, joy,** *and* **Jesus.** *Jesus came to bring hope, to heal, to bring new life, and to fill us with joy. Why shouldn't the church exhibit the same during Christmas at Oasis? We get to see lives changed because of it.* —PG

A World Record

Commit to the LORD whatever you do,
and he will establish your plans.

—Proverbs 16:3

I've always admired those who break world records. In fact, I've seen them as superhuman. Where did the thought come from? I want to attribute it to the Holy Spirit, but I am not sure He would want anything to do with it. I pray about everything, and if God gives me peace or does not close the door, then I will move forward if it is going to advance the kingdom work we are doing. However, as I mentioned before, this idea just seemed to form in my head during a sabbatical.

Oasis Church's world records for the most live lit trees (more about that in the next chapter) and the most nativity displays in one location are a tribute to hundreds of men and women who sacrificed their time, resources, and nativities.

When I suggested the idea of going for the record for the most nativities displayed in one place, no one liked the idea or thought it would work. The record at the time was somewhere over 900, and the most we had had was about 700. When you add in the work to set it all up, it seemed impossible to everyone with whom I shared the idea. Debby Brown was the one who would have to pull it off, and, while she was a leader and go-getter, asking her to do this was a leap.

I hardly got the idea out of my mouth when Debby said, "Let's do it!" I wanted to explain all the pitfalls and how I wasn't sure it was possible, but she kept saying "Yes, let us do it. We can do it. I got this!"

Debby's mother, Sally Rogers, had led our nativity display for years. She was a long-time Oasis member who had a deep love for this outreach and had taken the display well beyond anything I had dreamed. It was up to over 700 borrowed nativities when she had to retire because of cancer. She passed away shortly after. Then God did an extraordinary thing: He led her daughter, Debby Brown, to pick up the mantle. Because of her love for her mom and her mom's love for this outreach, Debby agreed to lead it. She jumped at the idea of reaching a world record for the most nativities displayed in one place. Our first world record would have never happened without her.

Debby took this project on with a vengeance and made it happen. She was creative and tenacious, and she got the entire church involved, along with others in the community. She even had our children's ministry making homemade nativities. That was genius because it involved the next generation as well.

Then we found out the 900 figure was an old one and that the current record was more than 1,800. I thought that would be a deal breaker, but Debby said resolutely, "No, we will do it."

It was touch and go until the night of the counting. Many hours were involved just to get the attempt approved by Guinness. That might have been the hardest part. The paperwork and the months of waiting for approval were stressful, but Debby kept at it until it happened.

Then, when we finally got to the day, there were so many guidelines to be followed. It had to be documented by outsiders, experts, and even journalists. The details were overwhelming, and the only person who understood them was Debby. She organized people, teams, and ministries. She owned it and believed in it with all her heart.

Those who lead must build teams around them, or their projects will never be enough to draw anyone's attention other than members and friends. We would never have achieved two world records without a Debby and her team.

The record we set was 2,150. The plaque hangs in our lobby beside the Guinness record for 546 live lit trees.

Doing something big like this is worth it. First, it gives your church a big goal to go after, and people love being a part of something bigger than themselves. Second, it gets exposure. We have always had some TV or newspaper coverage but nothing like the coverage we had for the Guinness records. At least one news outlet is a requirement. The exposure for your community is invaluable. We could never afford to pay for the coverage we received for the two records. Third, it reminds your community you are there. You build goodwill, and the community realizes you are going above and beyond for them. If they like you, they will be more open to your message. I am not talking about compromising your message or convictions for the world's adoration, but it is not a sin for the community to like you. Fourth, it propels the rest of your Christmas display, and it fuels your outreach year-round. When people get ready to visit a church, you are at least on their minds. People in your community will think of you when they get ready to visit at Easter because of your Christmas outreach the previous year. Last, it gives you something to celebrate year after year. It adds credibility to your display with those who are new in the area and were not here when you achieved it. Every year we highlight our two world records as we promote our Christmas display.

We no longer do the large nativity display. With the other activities we provide, a lack of space, and our desire to highlight our children's ministry, we need the auditorium space, so we share it now. Each year we incorporate about two hundred nativities since that's a huge part of our history.

On any budget, you can reach thousands of people at Christmas. Even as a new small church beginning in a trailer, we had started to reach thousands during the Christmas season with simple lights and some metal-lit displays. There are few stories out there like ours, and I wrote this book in the hope and prayer that there will be more.

A church I visited years ago in a mountain community of North Carolina touched several communities with their light display. I heard about them through the company where we bought lights and drove out there. I found out the church was not even in a community; it was out in the middle of nowhere. But hundreds of people would come out to see the church lights during Christmas, and the church was well known in the surrounding communities. If this little church could be visited by several thousand people in the middle of nowhere, then why couldn't we?

For many years, I have traveled to visit light displays around the country during the holidays. Each time I learn things and get ideas and new inspiration. I cannot count how many displays I've seen over the years. Sadly, only two were at churches. There must be more, but I have yet to find them. Many churches decorate, but they do not use inexpensive yet effective visuals. I am frustrated and amazed by this truth. I want so badly to see churches making a difference in their community.

I could pastor any church anywhere, and I would do what Oasis is doing today. I am passionate about Christmas. I love what it stands for and how our Savior can change a person's life and destiny. Sadly, the way we celebrate Christmas as churches is mostly traditional and not that biblical. The church must not only embrace Christmas but also share it with our lost communities.

THE POWER OF A STORY

Being Part of God's Narrative
From: Ricky Garcia, Executive and Administrative Pastor

Ricky is the glue that holds our team together. As our executive and administrative pastor, he leads our staff and our key leaders. Ricky is not the biggest fan of Christmas. He did not come to Oasis for CATO. In fact, I would say he might not have come if he had known. We joke about this all the time, but I think it is true. Just as Ricky goes full steam into everything he does, he also is a team player and expects it of each member of our team. I could not be writing this book or doing the things I do as a senior pastor without Ricky. He is not the key person of Christmas, but his leadership is what allows us all to be able to do CATO. He did not grow up at Oasis, but you would never know it by his love for our church family. I think CATO has grown on him, since he is willing to do anything that brings someone to Christ. —PG

My first experience of Christmas at the Oasis was not as a guest but as a staff member. A couple of things impacted me the most: I have a great appreciation for the heart behind CATO, which is to offer light, hope, and joy to the community. I definitely love how the property on the corner of 14th Street and Flamingo is maximized to light up the community that surrounds it. I have had many different roles every year I have served at CATO, but being at the exit as folks leave the event is so special. Hearing them saying thank you and how much they enjoyed the event really warms my heart. It warms my heart because it lets me know that we accomplished what we set out to do, which is to be a light within our community and in the lives of those who live in it. One powerful story I can't forget happened in 2019. I was directing traffic one evening, and a congregant who had not been attending very long approached me. At first, I was concerned for his safety because he was walking among moving cars, but he asked if he could share something very quickly with me. So, I found someone to cover for me for a couple of minutes and we moved out of the vehicle pathway. This gentleman went on to share that he had sat through one of my sermons a couple of weeks prior to that night that had encouraged him and had given him the strength to step out of the depression he was fighting. He was there at CATO that night with his wife and kids and had this big smile, as if five tons of weight had just been taken from him. This was another moment that reminded me that CATO is so much more than lights, trains, or hot cocoa. I truly was a part of the narrative that God was writing in the lives of every person who experienced CATO.

I can describe countless faces who come on our property during CATO and the bliss that I see as they take in every display and activity. But nothing can compare with what I see God doing through our staff. I get to witness the miracles happening in the kitchen. I get to witness our staff pour out everything they have to create an experience that will impact thousands of people they may never meet. They go at it fervently and work hard to create the best experience possible. I love watching their faces as they see the guests take in the fruits of their labor. This is CATO through my eyes. I am always grateful to be a part of the story that God is writing.

*Ricky's story is different, but note how every part of it is around our mission. One thing Ricky mentioned is the hearts of our volunteers and staff. When a man needed to speak with him, he stopped what he was doing and took the time. Sometimes it is stressful when several thousand people are all over our little property during CATO, but each member of our team will always stop and meet someone, pray with them, hear their problems, and take the time to do whatever they may need at the moment. They are selfless and more concerned about **the one** than the task. That might be the biggest difference between other public events and commercial tourist parks. It's not an event, it's a ministry, and Ricky does it as well as anyone. —PG*

Drive-By to Leader
From: Valentina Rueda, Former Office Staff

Val is a passionate follower of Christ and one of the sweetest people I've ever known. But don't mistake her sweet countenance, smile, and winsome spirit for weakness or shyness. She has great strength and has faced more adversity than most young adults of her age. She is a tenacious fighter for what she believes, and I know God has great things in store for her and her husband, Alan. They happened to be newlyweds at the time I was writing this book. While Valentina does not serve on our staff team during this season, she is a valued active member of Oasis Church.
—PG

I remember coming to Oasis Church to see the lights during my middle school years. It became an annual family tradition. Even though my family attended a different church, we were always on Oasis Church grounds during the holidays. We had come across this amazing community opportunity simply by driving by. One night we were driving down Flamingo Road and gasped at the sight of an entire church building lit up in blinking string lights. I don't even remember what we were doing out that night, but we didn't go through with our original plans. We immediately pulled over and parked to see what this winter wonderland had to offer. My younger brother and I ran all over the campus oohing and aahing at the beautiful light displays. We were most shocked at the smiling faces all over, offering hot chocolate and s'mores. We left feeling happy and filled. I remember going almost every week during December. Years of this tradition passed until my high school years. We had no church home at one point for a variety of reasons, but in December of 2013, we found ourselves doing our annual festivities at the Oasis Christmas celebration. We stood outside and my parents asked each other, "Wait, why haven't we attended a service here?" That following weekend we attended a service and felt at home. Now I have an incredible church family and have even served on staff. My story is only one of the ways that CATO impacts our community. As a member of Oasis now, I get to see the beauty on people's faces every year. People of all ethnicities and beliefs visit us during CATO, and this opens an opportunity to impact their lives with Christ.

If I had a dollar, as the old saying goes, for every person who's mentioned how they first would drive by and see the lights before deciding to drive onto our property, I would be a rich man. Val and her wonderful family have been a gift to our church, but unfortunately, her family had to move back to Ecuador a few years ago and leave Val here. I love that most every Sunday I see her family worshiping with us from the mountains of Ecuador. We are still family even though we are not worshiping in the same building. This past year, Val and Alan were our volunteer photographers for CATO. Having their own professional photography business allowed them to donate their remarkable expertise to the body of Christ at Oasis through CATO. —PG

CHAPTER 8

Propelled by Missions to Another Guinness World Record

"And you will be my witnesses in Jerusalem, and in all Judea and Samaria, and to the ends of the earth."

—*Acts 1:8*

How did one mission outreach propel us to another Guinness World Record? You now know our story of how God expanded Oasis from a small church of less than 200 to over 2000, and through CATO's 25 days, it reaches up to 52,000 people yearly on our property through a simple Christmas light display. I think the best part of CATO is not even what happens on our property or the hundreds who have come into our Oasis family on this little six acres on the corner of 14ᵗʰ Street and Flamingo Road. There is so much more to it than meets the eye. And in the past ten years, the expanded missions that Christmas has created at Oasis have become the dearest thing to my heart.

While missions have always been one of our three values (worship, community, and missions), it was probably the slowest one to develop when we were a young church struggling to build a foundation in our community. I have always had a heart for missions. As a child, I was taught to give above my tithe of 10 percent to missions. I grew up in a very mission-minded church and was constantly exposed to missionaries and mission projects. I have many times stepped out in faith and pledged to give money I did not have to missions. One year as a teenager, I was working as a part-time janitor for my home church in Hollywood. Through an honest mistake, they had messed up my paycheck, and the IRS made them make it up. I wasn't the only one who received an inaccurate paycheck. One of our pastors who was leaving to move to the tundra of Wisconsin did as well. God laid on my heart to give the entire amount of my check to help that church planter, who was making great sacrifices to start a church.

One year Tonia and I gave up our daily newspaper so we could give more to missions. The paper was as valuable to us then as social media and online news are today since there was no other way to get the news except on TV. Giving up our newspaper was huge, but I felt compelled as a young husband and father to do whatever we could to support missionaries and their calls. One year we cut our cable to increase our giving to missions. Even living on a shoestring budget and at times not knowing where our next meal would come from, we always felt compelled to give to those who had given up so much to go serve others. Why do I say these things? I want you to know that missions have always been a big part of my life personally.

When we planted the new church that would eventually become Oasis Church, one of my goals was to be a mission-minded church. But for some reason, other things would get in the way. We would periodically support a missionary we knew and do the occasional outreach, but it always seemed totally inadequate and woefully short of our missions' value.

Adding to this, the church was becoming more diverse by the year. But why were we putting off asking our people to support missionaries, total strangers, over and above their tithes and offerings?

Most of our people had come from countries where we have always sent missionaries. A friend of mine, Ken McCord, while we were flying to Brazil to visit his dad, Bud McCord, a pastor sent from the Hollywood Church, opened my eyes as never before.

As a missionary kid, Ken understood the difference in cultures better than I did. From that conversation in the middle of the night, 35,000 feet over the Caribbean, a light switched on. Our church is the world. The world has come to us, and what began with eighteen countries in our early years had mushroomed to over ninety countries that our people had migrated from. Why not use this as the basis of our missions? That is a great story, and this is not the place to share it all, but I will say my goal is to one day have missions going on in every country our people are from. We are slowly moving in that direction.

As our missions' emphasis grew, our team saw that we had so many people coming onto our property, and yet it was all about the traditional four walls. We needed to figure out how to leverage all these people to make an impact with those hurting in our community and around the world.

CATO gave us the launching pad to not only support missions endeavors but also to help others. Through Christmas at the Oasis, we have taken offerings of money, food, and other items to send to the Caribbean islands after hurricanes. We have done toy drives for one of our long-time partner ministries in South Florida, Sheridan House Ministries, which serves hundreds of single parents. Some years we've set up semi-trailers for donations to missions' projects. Our biggest outreach is Bike for Haiti, which has been featured during Christmas in various ways. Money has seldom been taken up, but there are so many other ways we can do missions through community events like Christmas.

Seventeen years ago, my wife, Tonia, had a burden to have the women's ministry house the homeless at Christmastime. December is a tough month for the shelters in our area, and they are always in need. When it gets cold up north, homeless people stream into South Florida, adding to the numbers of those in our area without a place to live.

One of the Christian homeless ministries in our city called Faith in Action does a wonderful job of providing temporary shelter. Tonia reached out to them. In December they ask churches to house up to five families on the premises for a week. For the last fifteen years, we've done that. We call it Homeless Week. The families that stay with us are so grateful. Our people smother them with love and gifts during that week. We shower the kids with Christmas presents, and we treat them to a special night at Christmas at the Oasis.

Homeless Week has become known as an opportunity to show dignity to those staying with us that week. We have limited facilities; that is a major challenge, and we only have one shower in our entire building. The families sleep on air mattresses in our various children's rooms. Our ladies' ministry treats them with huge home-cooked meals, gifts, and activities for the children. Some of these families come back years later to attend Oasis or to thank us. Homeless Week allows this church in the suburbs to serve the poor and hurting as Jesus would. It's a lot of work, but it's one of the most fulfilling mission outreaches of Christmas at the Oasis. Many of our families can't wait each year to serve these families in Jesus's name.

We've had a different missions outreach project each year. For Oasis, Christmas has become as much about missions as evangelism to our community.

One of the best mission outreaches we ever did was Trees of Hope, which I mentioned earlier in the book. It started nine years ago. We had been doing various mission projects, but I wanted something to serve our hurting community and make a Christmas tradition at the same time.

The genesis of Trees of Hope was my own experience, as I mentioned earlier when I shared my story about getting the last tree on the lot on Christmas Eve when I was a child. I thought, *Why not give other families the chance to have a live tree at Christmas?*

The Christmas tree is only a tradition, and we do not try to spiritualize it, but most people love a live tree. So, we began to buy trees wholesale from North Carolina tree farms. We provide approximately 250 trees to families who are out of work, hurting financially, or going through other hardships. Their names are provided by our church families and other mission partners in our community. On a special night set aside for them, usually before the week of Thanksgiving, we open the campus and offer them the CATO experience before it opens officially. A ton of volunteers strap trees to their cars and give them sets of lights for the trees and a tree stand. We learned early on that it creates a dilemma for the family if they have to go buy lights and a tree stand. We buy the lights and the stands after Christmas during the sales, and hardly ever pay full price. Generally, we find a bounty after Christmas at deep discounts. Our church members sponsor the trees each year and cover the entire cost, including the lights and stands.

This outreach is one of my favorites, and we get more feedback from it than almost anything else we do. As the families line up around the buildings the night of the giveaway, volunteers talk to them, offer hot chocolate, and make them feel special. Below is one recent story.

THE POWER OF A STORY

Tears of Hope
From: Yami McLaughlin, Assistant Business Manager

Now I want to introduce you to Yami McLaughlin. This young mother is probably one of the most mission-hearted people at Oasis. She organizes several foreign mission trips each year and gets involved in almost all our local mission outreaches. She's busy—she works for Oasis in our business office, runs her own tax service, and is a mother of three. This is one busy mom, but she always finds time to serve others. —PG

This is one of my favorite stories about Trees of Hope. At Christmas of 2019, a gentleman named Ernesto came to Trees of Hope to pick up a Christmas tree. He arrived in a minivan, and while he was waiting, he rolled down the window and we began a conversation. I quickly realized he had five children in the car. He then shared that he and his wife were foster parents with 4KIDS of South Florida, and they had a total of eight foster children at home. Ernesto was truly moved by the generosity of Oasis in providing a real Christmas tree for his foster family. Some of his children had never experienced that before, let alone a true family Christmas. Ernesto kept asking questions about why and how we do what we do. He was overwhelmed to the point of tears as he shared his story. He and his wife struggled to provide for their family despite the help they currently received. I could never forget his tears of joy and gratitude in awe of Oasis's thoughtfulness and generosity. "These lights, this small gift brings so much hope to us this Christmas," he said as he left.

That could have been my family, growing up, in that car. The same thread of hope and love is in almost every story. That's why we call it Trees of Hope. —PG

In closing out this chapter, I want to give you the cherry on top of this amazing outreach at Christmas.

When we started buying trees wholesale from a farm in North Carolina, we decided to buy up to one hundred fresh-cut trees to put around the property and to bring a little smell of Christmas to our campus. Some we even put in our lobby or sanctuary. The lit trees bring so much to our property, and the smell is heartwarming.

We had already won a record several years earlier for having the most nativities displayed at one time. But then we found out about the record for the most live lit trees in one location, and we decided to break it. It took 546 live lit trees, but we still hold that record. It is always fun to have a challenge. I don't think I ever heard of a church that has two world records. We never started out with that as a goal, but we again leveraged the Christmas outreach and made it far more doable. We have also seen some good press coverage of the records. Local press always covers a world record; our nativity record received even national attention. This kind of goodwill in our community can't be bought—it must be earned. We have spent almost thirty years earning it and continue doing so each Christmas. CATO gives us so many opportunities to share Jesus because of our credibility and goodwill in the community.

Who would have ever thought our missions endeavors would wind up in Guinness World Records? God is amazing when you take your little and give it to Him.

Tired, Overworked, and Overwhelmed

I can do all this through him who gives me strength.

—Philippians 4:13

A Christmas display like the one we do at Oasis Church will enlarge your ministry and effectiveness for the kingdom and our Lord. Once you understand the basics, there are some quick ways to start.

First, buy a couple thousand lights, which is only about twenty strings. We do mostly LED now, but they are more expensive and are not necessary. You can start with an inexpensive box of 100 lights, but if you can buy more, you should. The more lights you string around your property, the more attention you will draw.

Do not go for the perfect architectural lines. I would dare say that the displays you have seen over the years with lights and gaudy figures stuffed over every square inch were probably your kids' favorites. Decorate to attract the kids, not the adults. If you attract kids, the adults will come. Most adults attend our light display for their kids or grandkids, not for themselves.

As you build your display over the years, you can begin to go for impressive displays that attract adults too.

Don't wait until you have it all figured out. Get a few people and begin to hang lights. Your desire for perfection and fear that you will not get it right will keep you from doing anything.

Encourage your people to pick up an extra string or two and tell them the color you want. Spread the involvement out, and you will also spread out the ownership of the outreach. Some may buy a lot, but most people can afford a string or two of lights.

There are some drawbacks to having donated lights. There are many types, and you need to be careful how you hook them up.

Look for the locations that are most visible to people driving past your church. Don't think you have to start at the front door.

If you commit to this process and stick with it year after year, your church will embrace it. It is so much easier to get them excited about hanging lights and putting up decorations for their neighbors than beating them over the head to invite neighbors to a service or share the gospel with them. Nothing gives our church family a greater opportunity to share Jesus and the story of Christmas than inviting friends to Christmas at the Oasis.

Print up a simple invite, turn on the lights, and encourage your congregation to invite their friends.

Christmas displays should have the end goal of sharing the gospel with people who do not know Jesus, people who would never otherwise enter your church property.

At Oasis we annually remind the church of the real reason we do Christmas. The new people also need to get it. They need to invite their family and friends because they have a new circle of potential Christ followers. If they are new Christians, they are looking for ways to share Jesus, and this will make it easier for them.

If you attend or lead a larger church, you can do far more a lot faster. I would recommend you reallocate some of the local missions or outreach budget to decorating, lighting, and other endeavors that would make your property welcoming to your community.

Whether you have a small or a large church, you may have someone who can build the light displays. We have never had that many members who worked with their hands, and that has been frustrating when it comes to Christmas decorations. But it also makes anyone who does work with their hands invaluable. You can do more faster and with less expense.

Think of the Christmas decorations you can buy or make, like snowmen, sleds, candles, wisemen, angels, snow, trees, trains, wreaths, and so forth. Trees that people want to get rid of work great outside with lights. They look good at night in the dark. If you have someone who is a good organizer and can visualize where to put them, sign them up as your designer. Make a simple map on a piece of paper. We started with just hand-drawn maps that we sketched out in minutes. (Our first few years we even sketched our displays out on a napkin.) Now our team puts together a detailed blueprint. But you can start small. When people are used to driving by your dark property at Christmas, it does not take much to get their attention with a couple thousand lights and some displays.

One of the best ways to attract attention at a low cost is with blowups. Small ones can be bought for little expense. Look for larger ones after Christmas when they are on sale. The awesome thing about the blowups is that they take up a lot of room. We use them to fill in areas where we are short of other things. Children love them.

We buy most of our lights and decorations after Christmas. We don't try to be picky when buying during the sales. Sometimes the things we buy stay in storage for years until we figure out where to use them. We could never have done so much without buying at huge discounts.

We do make an exception for our wall of lights, which circles the auditorium and is synchronized to a music show. It is complicated and computerized, and it calls for more expensive lights and digital equipment. It is the biggest leap we've ever made, but we did not start it until we had been doing Christmas for twenty years and had thousands of people coming. The wall of lights was created by Joel Collins, a former staff member who called it the "wall of doom" because it was such a huge undertaking. If you are going to do something like that, I recommend going to a Christmas expo with the guys who will build it. But it's not something you need to attract your first guests to the property.

I hope you can see how easy and simple it is to reach thousands of people with a Christmas display. You can start one even if you don't announce it first. People will notice, and then you can build on the small beginning. Ministry is a journey, not a sprint. The same principles apply to a Christmas display.

Be aware that results may vary from church to church. It is not about duplicating what *we've* done but doing what fits your church. Remember that the displays are for the unchurched, not for Christians who want an inexpensive place to go during this special season. They are welcomed, but they are not the audience we focus on.

THE POWER OF A STORY

The Man Who Can Do Everything
From: Ron Orsini, Facilities Director, Deacon, Lay Pastor Chairman, Conga Player

Ron is the person that every organization, business, and church needs. He is a rare find and one who once again started at Oasis as a person sitting in a service when God touched him on the shoulder through one of our leaders. I could write a chapter on all the things Ron has done as a layperson and now as our facilities director. He continues to serve in our worship, student, and Cuban espresso ministry. —PG

My first recollection of Christmas at the Oasis is back in 2009 when Pastor Roberts asked me to build a Christmas village in front of the sanctuary under the west canopy. We also set up the skating rink there that year. My next year, I built Christmas tree arches. Next were the ticket booth and train-crossing lights. I built the toy soldiers the following year. Since 2015, I have been building the Christmas villages, including the gazebo, train depot, and barn. In 2016, I made the Bike-for-Haiti display and set up the trees at the entrance. Throughout these thirteen years, I have enjoyed the help and fellowship of an incredible group of men I call brothers. What makes me happy is listening to and watching families as they enjoy the experience I helped create. All for the one!

Ron mentioned several key things. The community of men he has developed are now brothers and co-laborers. This is huge; he doesn't do it by himself. This is a good lesson for all of us in ministry who think that if we don't do it, it won't be done right. He also mentioned Bike for Haiti, our largest missions outreach as a church, to which we have given over $750,000 over the last ten years. —PG

All Are Welcome
From: Luis Cardona, Creative Director

Luis first attended our church as a teenager with his mom. Through the years, he developed a passion for video, and a few years ago we hired him full-time. What was once a ministry anyone could do with a simple video is today a lynchpin of modern ministry. We could not do ministry without video. Luis's ministry extends to thousands outside our four limited walls via video. His story is very personal yet drives home one of our values since we began in September 1991: All are welcome. —PG

I have a homosexual brother who has always been super hesitant to go anywhere near church because he feels like he's going to be judged. During CATO, I got a phone call from him asking if I was at work and if he could stop by. I told him to pass through, and he ended up spending two hours on the property looking at all the lights, even sitting in through Jingle Jam, our Oasis Kids' Christmas play! After leaving, he called, thanking me and telling me it was the first time he'd ever felt welcome in a church. Since then, he asks me to pray for him occasionally and is a little more receptive to hearing about God (emphasis on "little").

Success! This might seem like a simple story that does not have the normal conclusion of someone coming to Christ, joining Oasis Church, becoming a fully devoted disciple of Christ, and then becoming an Oasis leader. But this is a beautiful story. It shows just how powerful Christmas lights and decorations are. Everyone enjoys them. We have atheists come through who love our lights, even with all the spiritual emphasis, the plan of salvation, and Bible verses in the displays. Remember the Jewish person who got the nativity thrown out of the mall? Well, into the first few years of CATO, we felt that since we had thousands of Jewish neighbors in a large condo community across the street, we would also make a display that honored their holiday of Hanukkah, which usually falls around Christmastime. Hanukkah, a celebration of lights, fits perfectly with the celebration of Jesus, the light of the world. We proudly put the Hanukkah candle display in a very noticeable place so our Jewish friends would see there is a place for them. Most every year we have at least one phone call or letter thanking us for including the Jewish people in our Christmas celebration. That's a far cry from the mall controversy. —PG

Little Budget, Big Impact

"If you can?" said Jesus. "Everything
is possible for one who believes."

—*Mark 9:23*

When a staff member wants to do something new, my first question is, "What will it cost?" After four decades in ministry, I have watched pastors crash and burn after leading churches into debt, sometimes killing the church. While I love to dream and think big, I am very conservative when it comes to spending money. Our overall ministry and mission could be hindered if we pay for a good idea with money we don't have.

It is almost impossible to give one-size-fits-all budgeting advice, except to say to prayerfully move forward when it comes to creating a financial plan for your Christmas outreach. You can have a big impact in your community on a small budget. In the previous chapter, I laid out how to start small, but not every church has to do that. Your church may be large and able to allocate money from another outreach. You may be able to begin big from day one.

At the end of this chapter, you will find a QR code that will take you to our website and some samples of our Christmas budgets through the years. They will help you visualize what I have been saying: every situation is different.

Your church can do a community Christmas outreach and potentially reach more people than you have on Sunday morning. But do not get hung up on what you don't have—look at what you do have. Your people are your best resource. You can leverage your location no matter where it is. The sample budget items you'll find on the website will give you ideas for the future. You do not have to begin that big unless your budget allows it.

As I mentioned earlier, we started CATO at no cost to our guests. But over the years, we have added many items to our display. These items go in our budget for five to seven years before we can even purchase them. I had budgeted our trains, for instance, for years before we got one. We charged a few dollars to ride this rudimentary train propelled with a garden tractor dressed up to look like an engine, and it was paid for within two years. It was so popular that we bought another one two years later, and a few years ago we added several more train cars to accommodate the crowds. I wish I could have taken this step earlier, but the initial $5,000 was just too much to spend without knowing whether we could recoup the cost. Looking back, it was an opportunity missed. Our trains provide approximately $7,500 each annually in cash that we can use for other events. We have even used them on special weekends to ferry families from the parking lot a block away to the buildings. It is a kids' favorite.

Other items are much cheaper but bring a big return. Next are some examples.

- Snow machines blow a snow-like substance. We have learned to make a solution that is more like a dish-soap mixture. Nothing gets kids more excited than when the snow-blowing machines come on in our snow village. It may be the most exciting interactive event we provide nightly. For a few hundred dollars, you can have snow.

- We have done both photo spots and booths. Years ago, we provided nativity costumes for families to have their pictures taken in a nativity scene. The lines got so long we had to discontinue it. Long lines can create ill will and have at times even led to fights breaking out. We do the photo spots now, the kind you see in amusement parks. There's no cost. We already have the lights and displays up, and a small sign denoting it as a photo spot makes it extra special. One great touch is to have a volunteer offer to take the picture for a family. Our guests love it, and it allows us to connect with them personally.

- Free snow cones, cotton candy, and popcorn were wildly successful and cost very little. The rent for the needed machines is low, or you can purchase them for a few hundred dollars. The ingredients are also inexpensive. The issue of ill will because of the long lines forced us to start charging for snacks and refreshments. That helped to control the line. We not only covered our costs but also made money to go toward our light display.

- Other refreshments are almost a must. We have not always offered them, and when we first started, we gave them all away. But that created other issues. People are used to paying for things, and you can make them very affordable. Our refreshments, along with the train rides, brought in approximately $45,000 in 2021, which helped tremendously toward the cost of all we are doing today. S'mores have become a big hit; the fire pit draws people to the snow village area. We bundle them up in baggies by the hundreds before beginning our display, and we cannot keep up with the sales. The costs must be included in the budget. Do not risk doing it all at once, and do not order too much. There is a high probability you will have leftovers sitting around the rest of the year. It would be better to run out and give them a taste of what is to come next year.

- Absolutes in budgeting include our electric bill. Many people think it is sky high, but it's not. We spend maybe 25 percent more in December than the rest of the year. The lights run for only about four hours a night. LED lights, if you can use them, cut the bill even more. There's more cost in adding electrical infrastructure around the property. One year, we had to invest about $25,000 on electrical outlets. It was a significant investment but well worth it. The cost of the GFIs is a big thing these days. A GFI is a safety feature for the outdoor outlets that trips the circuit if there is moisture. Rain is our enemy, and we hate it in December. It can shut us down quickly. We have also used generators, both rented and loaned, where we needed power.

- Security has turned into a significant budget item. We have a volunteer safety team of church members, but we hire up to three professionals for security, depending on the night and crowds. Doing this is necessary for us, but you will have to determine if you need it. Our safety team also helps with parking and directing traffic on the main road. If you start with just a simple drive-through where people are not parking, you likely won't need security. We also pay for overnight security because we have invested so much around our property.

- Advertising is a considerable cost for us. In the last few years, we have used only social media and saved about $20,000. But I still believe in bulk mail several times a year. If you do bulk mail, the printing is a major cost. This kind of advertisement alerts the community of your display and helps attract people early on. It also reaches newcomers in the community who might visit at other times. It is not uncommon for a visitor to say they received our Christmas mailing. Advertising helps, but it is not a necessity. Still, I am glad we do it. After so many years of doing Christmas, we find that CATO is now a tradition people look forward to. Also, a crowd draws a crowd, and your best advertising is word of mouth and media stories about the church. The smaller the community, the more this kind of advertising takes place. NOTE: This past year we did a special bulk mail to 100,000 homes of new families who had recently moved to the area. They also received a gift they could pick up at church if they brought the mailer and gave their name to us for future follow-up.

- We did CATO for about fifteen years before the city made us get permits. Once you reach a certain size, city officials notice. Every year we must apply, and the city inspects the property before we open. I hope you do not have to go through this. The first time they showed up unannounced, we had to shut down until we met the codes. It cost us twenty-four hours of working through the night and $10,000 in new electrical cords. As they say, you cannot fight city hall. It is unlikely they will bother you until people begin lining up on the streets and walking around your property. Make sure you meet regulations from the start. Getting a permit is not as hard as it seems; do not let that keep you from beginning a display.

- You may want to include big budget items. Consider buying in small portions each year, as we did with our metal light displays. We started buying about six a year. Now our display is so large for our small property that we seldom buy a new one. Displays currently can range from $150 to $5,000. They have gotten more expensive because you cannot add the lights yourself (lights are already built into the metal light displays). And they are LED, which inflates the price dramatically. But it is worth it if you can add one or two displays a year. Someone in your church may even be able to build your displays.

- A live nativity is one of the least complicated Christmas displays you can do and one of the most effective. The biggest draw is the animals, but we do not have many farms in our area, so it was costly for us. People come to see and pet the animals. They hear a prerecorded story about the birth of Jesus and the plan of salvation while feeding the animals. Before farms became obsolete in South Florida, we could rent animals for about $350 per night, so it got expensive when we did twenty-five nights. When we did it only on weekends, the cost became about $1,000 per night. That was not within our budget, and we did not feel it was worth continuing. But if you have farm animals in your area, you might be able to do it for a little or nothing. It is worthwhile if you can do it.

- The light wall is an animated wall that many people around the country do at their homes. Our animated wall was probably the most dramatic addition we did to take our display to another level. Thousands of lights surround our building on the walls, walkways, trees, and roof, all coordinated to a show of music. It is stunning to see them from the highway. You cannot drive by without noticing that something big is happening here. The light wall began with about a $15,000 investment, and by now we have probably put a total of $25,000 into it over the last eight years. That is still a modest figure, and we have tech guys who can do miracles within our limited budget.

- Special giveaways have always been fun. However, they can be expensive, so each year we weigh the practicality of doing them. Big hits include 3-D glasses and candy canes for everyone who drives through. All our giveaways combined can cost up to $5,000, depending on how many there are. We cap our giveaways at ten thousand items and label them "while supplies last." Candy canes are the cheapest giveaway you can do, and they are usually very inexpensive. Our team orders them now online far in advance, since many suppliers run out close to Christmas.

- We pay about $250 for a radio transmitter that plays music on the radios of cars driving around the property. We record a history of CATO and provide a tour as people drive along. We include invitations to our Christmas services, especially on Christmas Eve. We ensure that our print, digital, and live communications in December announce our Christmas Eve services. Many people look for one to attend even if they do not go to church regularly. Almost all the guests who attend our Christmas Eve services heard of them through invitations extended during CATO. We even used our radio transmitter (powerful enough for our property under FCC guidelines) to do our drive-in Sunday services during the first six months of the COVID-19 pandemic.

- One of our pastors, Pat Roberts, who led CATO for several years, proposed the idea of a skating rink after seeing one outside Disney World. It has been popular, but it's one of the most expensive things we do. The initial cost of the plastic that mimics ice is expensive, and then we have to buy the skates. If you live where ice rinks during the winter can be kept outside, it is a great idea, but it is labor intensive for volunteers and staff. You also need to have waivers and safety protocols in place, so do not try this on a whim. We charge a nominal fee to rent the skates, but if people bring their own skates, the skating is free. The cost to set this up the first year was about $10,000, which covered the liquid spray for the faux ice, the faux ice itself, the skate sharpener machine, and a few dozen different-sized skating shoes to rent. We recovered the investment in about three years.

- The Ferris wheel was something grand we did for our twenty-fifth anniversary. It was not only fun but also effective. People could see it from far away while driving down busy Flamingo Road, which is a state highway. It worked perfectly for the wow factor of our special anniversary. We worked hard to make the space for it, but it was a special occasion. However, we will not do it again. We charged for it, but the admission fees did not cover our costs. We do not regret doing it once because it was the focus of our entire property that year. When we began to get quotes, we found prices that ranged up to $150,000 for the month, much more than our whole budget. The pastor in charge of finding it finally discovered a fifty-year-old one for $25,000. That was a bargain. It was popular with our guests but not so much with our staff. We may not have covered the cost, but we came close. And the PR that came with it made it worthwhile.

- Many other items go into the budgets. When you plan your budget, you might consider souvenirs you can sell. These can be items like mugs, ornaments, lights, or Christmas toys that light up. We have done this, but we have not found a formula to recoup the money we have spent on it. The gift store idea has not worked well for us. I would not suggest trying it until you have a large number of visitors for your display.

We hope that the result of these budget items has transformed lives. Only in heaven will we know the extent of it.

THE POWER OF A STORY

Mrs. Christmas
From: Luann Willix, Christmas Director

As I write this, I realize there would have been no Christmas at the Oasis these past seven years without Luann, truly the consummate servant. I am not sure there has ever been a bigger servant's heart at Oasis. You will see and hear much more of her as we look at the nuts and bolts of Christmas because Lu is the one who makes it happen.

I must admit that even when she and her husband, Bruce, started attending our church over a decade ago, I almost immediately saw their servant hearts. What was not evident at first was her leadership ability. I have our executive and administrative pastor, Ricky, to thank for that. When the pastor who was leading Christmas left our staff, Ricky brought Lu's name to me. This may be the biggest job on our entire staff and certainly touches more people than any other all year round. Luann has led our Christmas to heights I have never seen or imagined would be possible. She does it with a passion, not just for Christmas but for the one, and these two stories show it. —PG

A Fly on the Wall

One of my favorite CATO stories comes from my second year of working at Christmas at the Oasis. At the time, I was also working a part-time job at a doctor's office. It was probably the second week in January, and I was bringing a patient into the room to wait for the doctor. Before I could leave the room, the nurse asked her how her Christmas was. Instead of leaving, I shrank into the background, hoping to become a "fly on the wall" listening to her story. The girl began telling the nurse that she and her dad had gone to this church in Pembroke Pines that had Christmas lights all around. Suddenly, I wished I could be a fly on the wall, as the saying goes! She proceeded to say how the holiday had been very difficult because her mother had recently passed away, but walking around the property looking at the lights was so peaceful. She said they stayed for several hours walking and talking, reliving wonderful memories of her mom. She went on to share that she truly believed it was the beginning of their healing process. At that moment I saw the true treasure of Christmas at the Oasis. By just being on the property, they felt Jesus and a love they had never felt before. It was at that moment, listening to this girl's story, that I realized the extent of my love for my church and how blessed I had been to be a small part of this outreach.

The Joy of a Child

As I was guiding people across the crosswalk, a family was strolling on the walkway. Suddenly, from the midst of the family, a little boy about five years old let out a loud squeal. I was trying to see what he was so excited about. Was it the lights on the trees? Was it the teenager across the way dressed like Elsa, from Disney's *Frozen*? Then, the little boy shouted, "Look, Mom! It is baby Jesus!" Across the street was a blowup of the nativity with baby Jesus. Oh, to have the joy of that little child seeking Jesus. I just stood there and thanked God for allowing me to be there at that moment and see this child's joy. I prayed at that moment that God would give me the same joy and wonder each time I see Jesus.

Don't you just love Luann's heart? Once again, you see the heart of an Oasis member who came as a volunteer and now is leading our largest outreach ministry, one who heard God's movement in the lives of others through our Christmas display. —PG

Nuts and Bolts that Make It Run

*Now it is required that those who have
been given a trust must prove faithful.*

—1 Corinthians 4:2

For your potential Christmas ministry to reach its heights, a ministry director is a must. Having a director devoted to a steadfast ministry is pivotal. Depending on the size and scope of your display, the work begins early in the year and culminates in December. The director of Christmas at the Oasis dedicates time to nurturing its kingdom impact. Not all directors will look the same, but a love for Jesus, people, and Christmas is key.

The ministry director doesn't have to be an expert in any particular field, though that may help. But a willingness to learn, adapt, and lead by example should be top qualities. This person dictates the look, feel, and tone of the ministry.

Q&A with Luann Willix, CATO Director
Interviewed by Katia Droira

Luann Willix is our CATO director, the brain who makes it run. We couldn't do this ministry year after year without her kind of leadership. We decided it might be helpful to anyone considering starting a Christmas display ministry to hear her story and perspective. It proves how God will mold and direct your leader if he or she is willing to listen.

With the energy of a million beams of sunlight and her disarming demeanor, Luann will be the first to tell you that she loves the Lord and Christmas as much as she loves people. For Lu, Christmas at the Oasis represents thousands of opportunities to plant seeds of the gospel. Her impact is felt across our property and by the thousands who experience the love of Jesus.

You started at Oasis Church as a volunteer. How did you get to know the Lord? —KD

My parents never went to church. When I was a senior in high school, I started dating a guy, and one day he invited me to a church banquet. After the banquet, I started going to their Wednesday youth service.

On April 1, 1978, the youth ministry had a picnic at the park. The youth director came up to me in front of everyone and said, "Luann, would you give your testimony?"

I said, "I don't know what you are talking about. What's a testimony?"

"When did you come to know Christ?" she said.

"I don't know that I know Christ."

The youth director was floored. She hadn't asked me this ahead of time, and she was embarrassed. But she pivoted and got one of my friends to give a testimony.

After the picnic, the youth director approached me and asked, "You've never accepted Christ as your personal Savior?"

"No one has ever asked me."

"Well, do you want to?"

I said yes, and from that point on, I became involved in church. I remained in the youth group, and as soon as I graduated, I became a youth leader—sort of like a leader in training. That's the story of how I came to Christ.

And you've never stopped serving at church? —KD

No. I've been a member of only three churches since I was eighteen. I only moved when God moved me.

To be the CATO director, I think you have to love Christmas. When did your love for Christmas begin? —KD

I can't pinpoint one moment. I think my parents always made Christmas special, even when we didn't have a lot. We never got big, elaborate gifts. If there was some special thing we wanted, we got that, but no matter what, they always made it special. I think that's where I got my love for Christmas. With my own family, we started our own traditions, and it grew from there.

You started as a volunteer. Then you became a per diem Kids Ministry worker, a pastor's assistant, and took on other roles. How did this journey develop? What milestones led you to become the Christmas at the Oasis Director? —KD

My husband and I started out at Oasis Church's North Miami Campus. I was an Oasis Kids' volunteer first. Then I became a per diem kind of employee. When the church closed that campus, I volunteered Sundays at the Pines campus in the welcome center.

Twelve years ago, Pastor Brown and his wife took me to breakfast. During the meal, he asked, "How would you like to come and help me with Christmas at the Oasis?"

I didn't have any clue what it was. My family and I had been a part of the North Miami campus, not the Pines campus where the Christmas celebration was held. But because I love Christmas, I said, "Sure! I would love to come and do it."

I didn't have a clue then.

So that's your journey to get into Christmas at the Oasis. What about becoming the director? —KD

That took seven years working under two different pastors. As we went along, I learned more and more and took more responsibility. However, I didn't have the freedom to do some of the creative things I wanted to do.

When the last pastor moved on and the CATO director position opened up, I don't think Pastor Guy (our senior pastor) even considered me for it. It was Pastor Ricky who came to me and said, "Do you think you could do this?" And I said, "Absolutely!"

Being the CATO director is a hard job—very labor intensive, especially at the point we are at now. I think if someone were to start new, my advice would be to not feel the pressure to start big. Start small if you need to. Start with lights on the bushes, or a couple of light displays, but find your comfortable starting point. Share with people who can be excited to do this with you. Set up a small table with Christmas cookies and chocolate and some string lights. You can cover a lot of stuff with string lights. Any size church can do it, but you need to know where to start.

Do you remember a time or a specific moment when you heard God calling you to do CATO specifically? Or was it one of those "God-assignments" that was given to you—you knew it came from God and had to do it? —KD

I've always said that God has given me little "God-winks," as I call them, to confirm I am doing what I am supposed to. Every year at Christmas at the Oasis, He "winks" at me on more than one occasion.

For example, I remember one night when 40 percent of the lights were out, and a lady who had been there commented, "There were lights out?" It was like God was saying, "You are doing what you are supposed to be doing. You are on purpose. Just keep going."

How do you think your journey from volunteer to ministry leader prepared you for this special calling? —KD

I've been in ministry a long time. That's the key right there: the word *ministry*. Through all my church experiences, I've always looked at any position I've held as a ministry, not just a job. Even when I was volunteering, I looked at it as a ministry. Some of it is just who I am, but I know I am doing it for the Lord. I don't look for any other recognition. I want to hear, "Well done, good and faithful servant." That's how I go about everything I do. So, I think my previous years of ministry, even though they were in different areas, gave me the organizational skills and other tools to run Christmas at the Oasis.

What do you think is the main purpose of CATO? —KD

The main purpose is the one person who would come to know Christ by seeing the lights. It's not about the lights but the experience. We hope there are thousands who come to CATO, but it is really for the one. If one person comes to know the Lord, the twelve years I've been doing it is all worth it. Just the one.

Another way you could look at it is that this is a way to draw people onto your property who would normally never set foot in a church building. A lot of times when people hear the word *church* (I've noticed this especially as I've gotten older), it seems like a bad thing and not a good thing. The Christmas lights take away the edge. They trigger something in adults that sends them back to their childhoods. For everybody, no matter what country they are from, the lights trigger those fond memories.

That is one of the important things because it gets them on the property. Then, once they are here, they are greeted with warmth and love, and they see a difference. Maybe a year or two years later when something happens to them, they will remember our church and think, "That seemed like a safe place" or "That seemed like a place where love was. Let me just check it out."

Why do you think you've had such consistent success in rallying volunteers for CATO? —KD

I hope it's because I invest in the people who are with me. I try not to just ask, ask, ask, but to also get involved in their lives and be there for them. I've had a core group of twelve to fifteen people from every age who have pretty much been with me the whole time. Some have moved or whatever, but I know there are twelve or fifteen I can call on. I hope that's because they know they can also call on me and I would be there for them.

For over ten years now, we have established Tuesdays and Thursdays from 6:00 to 10:00 p.m. as Christmas work nights in our designated Christmas room starting early in the year. Can you tell us more about these times? What makes them so special? —KD

Christmas work nights build community. There have been periods of time when we've done a little Bible study or a devotional on those nights. Sometimes it happens organically and sometimes it's planned. With a few exceptions, our volunteers come right after work, and even before my time, the church would provide some type of meal— sometimes a light meal, other times full-on dinner meals. Sometimes we have even enjoyed a homemade dinner.

We also get a lot of community service workers who are not even from our church. Oasis has been working closely with our county's diversion program for many years now. We registered to partner with our sheriff's department to provide supervised work that helps people work out their minor offenses and helps rehabilitate them so they can stay out of the judicial system. They get to do their community service by helping with other volunteers, and we keep track of their work time and report back to each individual's officer in charge.

They are here because of drunk driving or whatever it happens to be. I don't need to know that information. When they come in, I treat them like all the other volunteers. They'll say, "I have my papers." I say, "We can deal with that later. Come on in. Thanks for being here. I can use your help." A lot of times, organic conversations would come up. Mainly the first question that comes is "What kind of church is this?"

At the end, they usually say we are super friendly and things like that. Some of those people have ended up coming to church here and even joining. I see several of them back every Christmas.

One year, I had this young guy who had been out drinking and got a ticket. He worked for an esteemed heart doctor and was embarrassed when he came. I said, "Don't worry about it." He worked really hard and now comes back every year to see me. He brings his kids now too.

It's about building relationships, not just with the church people. That is what I hope our volunteers get from coming to CATO volunteer nights on Tuesdays and Thursdays: relationships.

So, CATO is so much more than twenty-five days in December? —KD

Oh, so much more. It really is.

Can you mention some major highlights over the last twenty-five years that were like turning points for CATO? —KD

In the beginning, the live animals were a huge hit. They made a big spike in our attendance. We had our middle and high school students fill the roles in the nativity, and people still ask for it to this day. Another hit was the nativity display in the auditorium. We'd done it for several years, but the world record year was another big spike.

One more highlight was adding the trains. The year we added them was a big milestone. Then there was the year we added the hot chocolate. We went from cookies to hot chocolate. Again, every year people ask where the hot chocolate is. I believe it's because of the experience. It doesn't have anything to do with the recipe. Honestly, it is just the experience. Another milestone was when we added the firepits. We now have s'mores. People love them. Here in South Florida, we don't have many houses or families with fire pits, so it's a big thing.

One change we made in terms of the lights was putting in the lighted archway. We even held a wedding underneath that archway.

Trees of Hope was another huge thing. We give live Christmas trees, a stand, and lights to families in need. It's not about the lights, really. It's not about the live Christmas tree. It's about reaching the community, showing them that we care about them. By receiving a tree, a stand, and lights, they can carry on those traditions with their families, even in hard times.

Can you tell us about some challenges you have been able to overcome during your time as CATO's director? —KD

The latest challenge would've been the pandemic, which everybody all over has dealt with. However, we were able to hold CATO even during the first year of the pandemic. We went back to the drive-through, and we were able to have the lights on. This corner of our community wasn't dark. Actually, we put lights on the trees back in April, and we lit up our little corner way before Christmastime so people were able to drive through. I love to see people walking around, and keeping them in their cars is not one of my favorite things, but at least we were able to keep a part of CATO going even then.

One of the constant challenges we face, especially here in South Florida, is the rain. Over my twelve years, we have been looking for ways to keep the lights on when it rains. It's hard in Florida because all of those products advertised to keep your cords dry don't necessarily work here because of the humidity. If you put the cords in those plastic things, humidity still develops. We have tried to wrap them in plastic wrap, but the humidity still gets them. A solution we finally found is just black electrical tape. Everything can be taped up, all the little holes. But this is just a God thing. We can't say when it's going to rain and when it's not. That is one obstacle that has been a constant challenge, but the pandemic was the biggest. There haven't been any too many other obstacles I can look at and say, "Gosh, that kept us from holding CATO this year."

Can you describe your approach to your yearly budget? —KD

Honestly, I hate the numbers. I start where we ended the previous year. I take what we spent and what we made from the previous year and try to project those results when I do my numbers for the next year. This ministry has grown over thirty years, so the budget is different from when it first began. A small church can throw out a few lights and have the same impact. But now we are a lot bigger. One of my goals during my years in charge has been to stay under budget every year.

In your planning, do you take into account the yearly meeting you have in January? —KD

In January we have a planning meeting. So, when something new is coming—for example, if we want to buy a train—we have to recognize that's going to alter our budget. So, the meeting comes first. But I go into the meeting with the numbers report of the year before, so we know what we've spent and can decide if we have room to do something else. We take into consideration the economy at the time and how important it is to this church to continue Christmas at the Oasis. So, whenever there's something new, we go back to the church council and say, "We want to do this, but we may not cover it in the first year."

When we added the train, I think we told them we'd cover the cost within three years. With the skating rink, I think it was five. So, the church council knows some projects might warp the budget a little. We do charge visitors a nominal amount for those activities.

For somebody who has not done anything like this before, how does faith play into the approach to the budget? —KD

Faith plays into the budget big time—especially if you are coming off a "bad year" when you didn't meet the budget. The next year, you still need to have faith. It is constantly staying in prayer and seeking God's leading. It's funny how in these January planning meetings the conversations are very cohesive. That shows me that we are still on the right track, that we are still doing what God wants us to do, and that this is something we are still supposed to be doing.

Even though you guys are coming with different ideas for same things? —KD

Exactly. It's so funny, usually an underlying theme comes out in the meetings, even though no one has talked to each other about it beforehand. We always do a wins and opportunities analysis, so we see that year after year. I know I'm doing what I'm supposed to be doing when at these meetings I can be with seven to fifteen people from the staff, and we're all on the same page. Also, sometimes at these meetings we don't plan for just that year. Sometimes it's a five-year-out kind of goal. So that also comes into play with the budget.

If you didn't have a cap on your budget, what would you add for next year? —KD

If I didn't have a cap on my budget? I want a hayride! I want a hayride so badly. You wouldn't think a hayride would cost that much, but it would because we would have to put gravel in our retention pond. I would love that.

I would also love to try to repurpose our skating rink into some kind of tubing hill. That's another thing.

And to have all LED lights.

If someone reading this book is sensing God's tugging to serve in a similar ministry, what advice would you give them? —KD

Do it! On any level, if you ever feel God tugging your heart to serve on a certain ministry, do it. But this one—some form of Christmas ministry—I could tell you blessings after blessings after blessings I've received by serving. I'm not a volunteer anymore; I'm a paid employee. But I've heard story after story from our volunteers. Just seeing those smiles on the kids' faces, the thrill of the snow, any of those things. But for anything, if you feel ever God's tugging, you definitely need to get plugged in somewhere.

If you were to title this journey with CATO in your life, what would you call it? —KD

Possibly, "The Most Amazing Twelve Years of My Life." I mean, it has been an experience. There have been so many "God-winks" in the twelve years. It is hard work, but when God shows up, He shows up in ways I could not have imagined.

So, do you think you'd title it, "The Most Amazing Twelve Years of My Life," or "God's Winks Through the Years"? —KD

Probably, "God's Winks Through the Years."

How Can You Not?

For we walk by faith, not by sight.

—2 Corinthians 5:7 ESV

Two years into the pandemic, we still had Christmas at the Oasis despite many challenges. We had over 35,000 guests each year during eighteen days in December, and not one COVID case was reported. It was stressful at first, not knowing if anyone would come and whether it would be received as well with protocols in place. But we stepped out in faith, and God blessed our faith.

That is the message of this book: Step out and see what God will do. It may not make sense and you might be scared, but step out anyway. There are so many in your community who need Christ.

Find a way to touch Christmas in a big way. God will do something big with your mustard seed.

At our last Easter celebration, many families that had visited us at Christmas came to the service. Our staff tell stories of people they speak with. We encourage each team member to speak to at least two people each weekend about the next steps in their spiritual journey. Whether it is salvation, baptism, giving, joining a community group, or serving, we talk about their journey. Repeatedly, we hear that many of their journeys began with Christmas at the Oasis.

I hope you have a glimpse of what a church can do to reach people during twenty-five days of December.

Our Christmas at the Oasis story continues. As long as I am senior pastor, we will continue to present Christ to our community every Christmas.

We have some new twists coming this year.

I have become a Christmas tree farmer and a member of the Tennessee Christmas Tree Growers Association. I hope that in five or six years, the trees we planted this year will be ready to cut. My goal is to eventually supply two hundred trees a year free of charge to families of South Florida through Trees of Hope. It might fail, or it might work, but it is worth a try.

My hope is to plant two hundred a year. This would not only continue our mission but also replenish and renew the trees we cut. It has already made a couple of neighbors incredibly happy that we are replenishing trees. So, I will cut a couple hundred trees but will replace them eventually with up to a thousand.

As I begin to wind down this story of our Christmas ministry, I am also excited to share something our staff has been working on: Christmas at the Oasis goes digital.

Our team has put together a website where people can see pictures, videos, news reports, budgets, and a host of other things online. There is a QR code with a password for this site in the appendix.

We cannot possibly keep this book updated with new stories and ideas for those who may want to pursue a ministry outreach at Christmas, so we hope the website will be a blessing. Our heart is to encourage and help other churches. This is a kingdom ministry; let us share it with one another.

Appendix

Follow QR code for more of CATO. Enter the password at the bottom of this page to access your
Changing Your Community in 25 Days website.

PASSWORD: **CYCin25D**

Guy Melton serves as senior and founding pastor of Oasis Church of South Florida in Pembroke Pines, Florida. He loves his diverse congregation from over 90 countries and has a passion to dream big for God's glory.

Pastor Guy has a passion not only for extending God's Kingdom through his love for international missions but also for living in a missional local community. During over 40 years of ministry, he has seen the impact of the love of Christ in the many thousands of people who come to Oasis Church every year. His heart's desire for *Are You Adding or Multiplying at Christmas?* is to share the good news that any church, no matter what size, can have a similar impact on their community.

Pastor Guy has been married for 47 years to his high school sweetheart, Tonia, and has three grown sons and four grandchildren. Even though he loves to travel, he is devoted to his slice of paradise in South Florida.

visitoasis.org